BROOKLYN ELEVATED

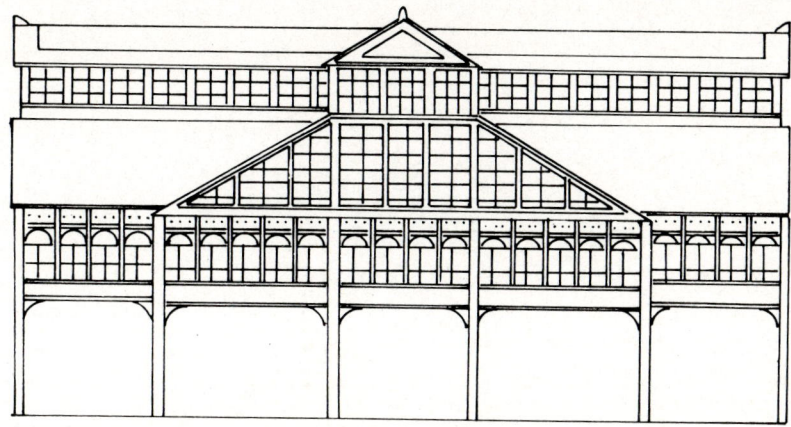

JAMES C. GRELLER & EDWARD B. WATSON

Dedicated to
Alexander (Pappy) Tatem

Published by:

N.J. International Inc.
77 West Nicholai Street, Hicksville, N.Y. 11801

1312 at Broadway and Myrtle, on the Myrtle El. Soon 1312 and her few remaining sisters will end the open gate era for the Brooklyn Elevated lines, as well as the whole country.

INTRODUCTION

The Brooklyn elevated system is part of the larger history of how everything changes. Part of the earlier elevated lines are still part of Brooklyn's transportation system today. Each step in the changes that were made for the Brooklyn elevated lines tells us something about what was happening to the land and its people in the boundaries of a place on the earth called Brooklyn. The early settlers took part in man's great invention, the steam railroad. People wanted to move faster from far away places like New Utrecht to Fulton Ferry, so excursion railroads sprang up. In the summer, vacationers now could make use of Brooklyn's great beaches. In 1883, a second great advance to Brooklyn and its transportation picture was the opening of the Brooklyn Bridge. The Bridge hailed the fact that Brooklyn had arrived. John Roebling, the Bridge builder had an idea that the Bridge would be very successful and provided it with a cable railway. From day one, the masses crossed the bridge and the little railway was the nation's shortest and heaviest travelled system. As the farms turned to bedroom communities, the once quiet five towns became one big city. Horse car lines and eventually, trolley lines were not enough to handle the loads to the Bridge. Railroads above the street were the answer, as they were in Manhattan and other cities. Again, several companies began to puff up and down the main avenues of Brooklyn. Workers from the Bushwick section could board a train headed for Sands Street station and change there to the Bridge Railway to continue to Park Row and the office. As the lines themselves populated the places between the Bridge and the Beaches, all these companies were merged into one efficient system. So like the trolley companies, the elevated companies became the great Brooklyn Rapid Transit Company or the BRT. Man's invention again would change the elevated system with the introduction of electric traction. Frank Sprague had made it possible to operate a number of electric cars together, multiple unit operations. It was a great task, but eventually some of the little Forney locomotives ran out their careers on sugar plantations in the south. The thrifty BRT would turn to their fleet of steam trailers for many of their new motor cars. The elevated lines reached their zenith till another invention, the subway proved a better idea. From the Edward B. Watson collection and others we tried to illustrate each of these important stages in the development of the BRT elevated lines. This is a great story and almost impossible to document all the various equipment changes and renumberings in print. What we have assembled will give the reader a good idea of a very interesting and successful form of public transportation. There are still a great number of people who had the opportunity to enjoy the great sensation of riding the lines and cars described here in. When a wood train of open gate 1300 series convertible BU's* would race into a station, a conductor striding two open platforms would pull back and open the gates. Once on board you perhaps wished to stay outside and ride the platform or sit inside next to fully open barred panels. Sit back in those yellow cane seats and with two bell rings by the conductor for the motorman, you were off. Soon the Brooklyn spring breeze would flow throughout the train as you passed over the roof from one neighborhood to another. For those of us who rode them, there is no ride on the system today that will ever come near the magic that these wood beauties could take us to.

*Term used for Brooklyn open gate car. It stood for the old Brooklyn Union Elevated Company.

STEAM TO

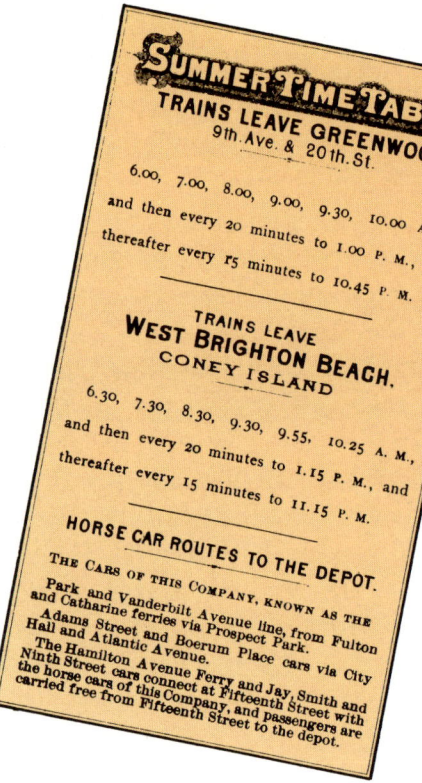

Many natural and un-natural things must come together for a city to be great, some too innumerable to mention but among the mentionable for Brooklyn is that it was blessed with a bountiful shore line. While Lincoln was still President, this growing city of shopkeepers, tradesmen, laborers, brewery workers and all their families were able to forget their toil and trouble and head to the beach. With the advent of steam, longer distances could be traveled more rapidly carrying larger crowds. To meet the growing demand of this summer traffic, a number of small steam railroads were built. These lines also carried local inhabitants and as the population grew, Brooklyn became the booming suburbs of its day and the area between depot and seashore grew into residential neighborhoods. Part of these lines are the basis of our rapid transit system today.

Among these pioneer steam lines are:

BROOKLYN, BATH & CONEY ISLAND, was opened in 1864 as a horse car line and soon converted to steam. The original route ran from 25th Street and Fifth Avenue to an amusement park in the West End of Coney Island and became known as the West End line. It was renamed the Brooklyn, Bath & West End in 1885, becoming part of the Nassau Electric in 1898. On February 16th, 1899 it became part of the Brooklyn Rapid Transit system. It was electrified in 1901 and elevated in 1917. Today one can ride over this route on the B train from Ninth Avenue to Stillwell Avenue.

THE SEASHORE

THE BROOKLYN, CANARSIE AND ROCKAWAY BEACH. Opened in 1865 from Atlantic Avenue and Fulton Street in East New York to the Canarsie Shore and from there by ferry to Rockaway Beach. It became the Canarsie Railroad, was electrified and leased to the Brooklyn Union Elevated (BRT) in 1906. It became part of the New York Consolidated Railroad (BRT) in 1912. Today one can ride the L line from Atlantic Avenue to Rockaway Parkway of the original route.

THE PROSPECT PARK & CONEY ISLAND RAILROAD. Opened in 1875 from the Culver depot in Coney Island to Ninth Avenue and 20th Street. This line was known as the Culver line, after Andrew Culver, its founder. This line was purchased by the Long Island Railroad in 1892 and was leased to the Brooklyn Rapid Transit in 1893, although the Long Island Railroad owned it and shared operation over the line until 1909. In 1899, the BRT and the Long Island Railroad reached an agreement by which the BRT would develop lines in Brooklyn only, with the exception of the Long Island main line and Atlantic Avenue while the Long Island would develop lines in Queens without competition from the BRT. The Culver line was electrified in 1899 and elevated in 1919. Today one can ride this Culver line on an F train from Ditmas Avenue to Coney Island.

THE BROOKLYN, FLATBUSH AND CONEY ISLAND. Opened in 1878 from the famous Brighton Hotel to Atlantic Avenue and Franklin Avenue connecting there with the Long Island Railroad. It became the Brooklyn and Brighton Beach Railway Company in 1887 and was merged into the Brooklyn Union Elevated Railroad Company (BRT) in 1900. It was electrified in 1899 and connected to the Fulton Street elevated providing through service to downtown Brooklyn in 1900. In 1905 the line was rebuilt to its present four track embankment and cut. Today one can ride this route on a D train from Prospect Park to Coney Island and the shuttle from Prospect Park Station to Franklin and Fulton.

NEW YORK AND SEA BEACH. Opened in 1879 from the ferry at 61st Street and First Avenue to the Sea Beach Palace Hotel in Coney Island. It became the Sea Beach Railway Company (BRT) and in 1912 merged with the Brooklyn Union Elevated Railroad (BRT) and the Canarsie Railroad (BRT) to form the New York Consolidated Railroad (BRT). It was electrified in 1898, rebuilt into a four track cut in 1913 and in 1915 was connected to the new Fourth Avenue subway to Manhattan. Today one can ride this route on the N train from Eighth Avenue Station in Brooklyn to Stillwell Avenue in Coney Island.

Ex-Manhattan Beach engine, now Long Island number #63 in 1888, at the curve at Avenue H. The locomotive was built by Rogers in 1883.

Brighton Beach train at the Company Depot at Fifth Avenue and 27th Street in 1876.

Propect Park and Coney Island's number Seven "Rosevale" was built by Baldwin in 1879.

Brooklyn and Brighton Beach No. 7 is an ex-Brooklyn Flatbush and Coney Island, built by Danforth and Cooke in 1879.

P.P. & C.I. loco number 6 at Coney Island Point (Nortons Point) in 1893.

The locomotive Stuyvesant posing on the narrow gauge New York and Manhattan Beach right of way in 1879.

(Top) Built by Baldwin for the Burnham, Parry & Williamson, the little engine was purchased and then rebuilt by P.P.& C.I. in December 1879. She is shown here in her official debut. (Top Right) Built by Danforth Locomotive Works in 1878, the Thomas Sullivan sure has a long boiler. (Center) No. 1, the Sea Beach started life as a Forney type when outshopped by Baldwin in 1877, but the Company rebuilt her into a 2-4-0 with a four wheel tender. (Bottom) Built by Baldwin in 1887, No. 3, of the B.B.E.W.E., looks cheated with a small four wheel tender that was popular with the Sea Shore Lines.

The East End began life at a narrow gauge engine for the New York and Manhattan Beach. The engine was rebuilt to standard gauge in 1883 and was sold to the Long Island Railroad in 1888.

The George A. Gunther was built by Baldwin in April 1871. This popular steam locomotive was dubbed a steam dummy type and used on horse car lines that converted to steam.

The brutish Forney type was built to haul the crowds to the Canarsie shore. Equipped with dual cow catchers to operate in either direction, the CANARSIE was built by the Rogers Locomotive Works.

Harry Colton leans on the cow catcher of the engine that carried his name in 1886 besides Greenwood Cemetery.

This aerial view of the eastern end of Coney Island will help place some of the islands interesting lines. The trestle is Brooklyn's first elevated as it crosses Ocean Avenue, the line is the Sea View Railroad. (Top) Sea View No. 3 was the island's smallest locomotive. It was built in 1879 by Baldwin for the Ninth Avenue El. It went to the Sea View in 1881. In the lower left can be seen the Boynton Bicycle Railway. (Lower Left) A close look at this 0-1-2 single rail engine shows how it was balanced from an overhead dual rail. These little lines connected the Brighton Beach Hotel and the Manhattan Beach Hotel with the Culver terminal (Right).

In the aerial view on the opposite page, the line in the foreground belonged to the Marine Railway that started as a narrow gauge, converted to standard gauge, electrified to center third rail then to overhead trolley wire. The Oriental is a duplex convertible car built by Brill in 1889. The panels lifted up into the roof. Finally in 1913 a storage battery car built by the Federal Car Company operated the line. The car will later go to the West Orange and Silver Lake.

What to do with steam open coaches at the advent of electrifing the lines was a problem. 3235 in 1899 was rebuilt into one big open bench car. It burned the same year.

3227 shows another West End steam open coach converted this time for elevated service in 1898. This car will last till 1905.

Posing at the J. G. Brill plant in 1877, No. 14 is a perfect example of the open excursion coach.

Passenger to Canarsie had fixed seats to ride on, in this no frills coach built by Brill.

Now Nos. 2 & 4 of the Marine Railway are more up scale with the storm curtains and classy paint job. They are a product of Jackson & Sharp of Wilmington, Delaware.

This early photograph shows a P.P.&C.I. coach of a fairly new builder from Philadelphia that will build many cars for Brooklyn, J.G. Brill. The longitudinal seating with a pot belly stove is what the local riders got during the off season. The subway lines still can give you the same seating arrangement today.

Jackson & Sharp turned out this spartan coach. With an interesting roof that is higher over the platforms.

13

Engine number 3 has just pushed a cable coach onto the Bridge cable for its trip over the Brooklyn Bridge.

BROOKLYN

14

BRIDGE

Manhattan Island in the 1870s to the 1880s grew to be the great commerical center that it still is today. A large pool of labor to run this great commercial city came from the City of Brooklyn. Ferry boats busy with the traffic, ever growing, moved them to Manhattan in the morning and home to Brooklyn in the evening. In 1883 a spectacular achievement that would change both cities for ever opened: The Brooklyn Bridge. John Roebling and his son Washington Roebling's great work made it possible for the multitudes to move in greater numbers more quickly from city to city, and they did. The Roeblings, being men of vision and in the wire business, provided for a cable railroad to operate from a terminal in Park Row on the Manhattan side to Sands Street on the Brooklyn side. The line opened on September 24th, 1883, only 6000 feet long but the traffic ranged from 40,000 to 225,000 passengers per day and from 1,000 to 20,000 per hour. Steam locomotives switched the cable cars at either terminal and would push them on to the cable section. In the late hours or when the cable was not in use these small locomotives would make the bridge crossing. The cable cars were electrified for lighting in 1894 by the use of a third rail and electric motors replaced steam in 1896. The motorman ran the electrified cars from a controller mounted on the front open platforms. The Elevated Companies (Brooklyn Union Elevated and Kings County Elevated) leased trackage rights over the bridge in 1897. By June, 1898, some Myrtle Avenue trains went to Park Row, while Kings County Elevate's Fulton El trains started service to Park Row by November, 1898. By 1900, the Brooklyn Rapid Transit operated the electrified line although cable continued to be used till 1908. After 1908, the cable cars being 10 feet wide (too wide for the El lines) were sold or scrapped.

New York & Brooklyn Bridge Locomotive Number One was built by H.K. Porter in Pittsburgh in 1884. (upper right) Number 12 shows that increased traffic called for heavier locomotives to move longer trains. These little engines spent a busy but confined life pushing cable cars on to the cable tracks and switching them at Sands Street and Park Row. When the cable was not in use, the engines ran with coaches over the Bridge. That must have been some ride.

(Far Left) In this photo a Brooklyn train arrives at the original Park Row Terminal in 1893. The Brooklyn bound track shows the area where the cable rises, that will pull a train across the bridge. The small tower would raise the cable so the coaches grip could pick it up. A steam engine would push a train to this point for the pickup. In 1902, a Manhattan bound train shows the electric third rail used by elevated trains, though the cable is still used. The Bridge also used a gauntlet track system to switch trains to the right platforms. (Lower Right) A two unit train of new 1300s leaves Park Row in 1905. You can still notice the cable that was used until 1908.

(Top Left) Park Row terminal changed a number of times to accommodate the overflowing traffic that persisted till the subways came. In the lower left, a Manhattan El steam locomotive can be seen.
(Above) The interior of the terminal has third rail for switching cars, no more steam locomotives. Platforms will later be put in on either side of the west end of the terminal eliminating the storage track shown in use in this 1900 photograph. The open portion will be enclosed.

(Left) New York & Brooklyn Bridge Railway car 102 with motormen on the open platform is coming into Sands Street terminal using electric third rail power.

Built by the Pullman Car Company at their famous Calumet shops, New York and Brooklyn Bridge 100 poses for the official photo. These were the first cars to be electrified. The controller will be placed on the open platforms. (Lower Right) The interior of 93 is of an earlier but similar car to 100. The photo is the official Pullman photo of 1891. The Bridge cars were among the most attractive of the elevated equipment. The end doors were extra wide double doors. The Bridge cars were too wide to be absorbed into the BRT fleet and were sold or scrapped. (Upper Right) Several went to the Mason City and Cedar Lakes and were rebuilt into interurban express cars. No. 19 is pictured in Mason City in 1950.

THE FIRST EL

Brooklyn Elevated Railroad's first train on Lexington Avenue May 13, 1885.

As was pointed out in the chapter on the Brooklyn Bridge the incredible amount of traffic to the City of New York could not be handled by the lines of horse cars to the ferries and later the Bridge. It was not possible for steam trains to run in the crowded streets so steam powered elevated railroads were the answer of the day. Steam locomotives could move more people faster via this bridge above the streets to other parts of Brooklyn. Later people from one neighborhood could shop in other parts of Brooklyn.

The first Elevated line was the Lexington Avenue elevated built by the Brooklyn Elevated Railroad Company and opened on May 13th, 1885 from Washington and York Streets to Broadway and Gates Avenues and later that year it was extended to Van Siclen Avenue in East New York. The Seaside and Brooklyn Bridge Company built an extention to Crescent Street/Cypress Hills in 1893 and it was later extended to 111th Street in 1917. The line was electrified in 1899.

Today the J train runs on this route from Gates Avenue to 111th Street. The Broadway Brooklyn line, built by the Union Elevated Railroad Company and leased to the Brooklyn Elevated Railroad Company, opened in 1888 to Driggs Avenue from Gates Avenue on the Lexington Avenue line. It was extened to Broadway Ferry in 1889 and later from Crescent Street to 168th Street, Jamaica in 1918. On May 30th, 1908 the line was extended across the new Williamsburgh Bridge to Delancy Street in Manhattan and further extended on August 4th, 1913 to Chambers Street under Park Row. Today one can ride the J train on this route from Marcy Avenue to Queens Boulevard.

The Myrtle Avenue line was built by the Union Elevated Railroad Company and leased to the Brooklyn Elevated Railroad Company, opened in 1888 from Grand Avenue to Sands Street. It was extended to Wyckoff Avenue in 1889 and to Metropolitan Avenue in 1906. It was electrified in 1900 and elevated from Wyckoff Avenue to Fresh Pond Road in 1915. Today the M train runs from Myrtle/Broadway to Metropolitan Avenue on this route.

Fifth Avenue line was built by the Union Elevated Railroad Company and leased to the Brooklyn Elevated Railroad Company, opened in 1888 from Park and Hudson Avenue to Atlantic Avenue. It was extended to Fifth Avenue and 38th Street by 1890. In 1893 an extension was built by the Seaside and Brooklyn Bridge Company to 65th Street and Third Avenue in Bay Ridge. The line was electrified in 1900. Only the Fifth Avenue, Culver portion of the F line from Ditmas Avenue to Coney Island remains today.

The Fulton Street line, built by the Kings County Elevated Railway Company, opened in 1888 from Fulton Ferry to Sackman Street. It was extended to Grant Avenue/City Line by 1893. In 1915, a final extension was built to Lefferts Boulevard. On July 9th, 1900, operation from Park Row to Brighton Beach was begun and remained in operation until the subway connection was opened for the Brighton line in 1920. It was electrified in 1900. Today one can still ride a part of this route on the A train from Hudson Street to Lefferts Boulevard.

By 1890, the Union Elevated was taken over by the Brooklyn Elevated Railroad. This merged company, the Brooklyn Union Elevated Railroad (in 1896, a holding company of the new BRT) acquired the Seaside and Brooklyn Bridge Company in 1899, the SeaBeach Railway in 1897, the Nassau Electric (West End) in 1899, the Kings County Elevated Railway Company (Fulton & Brighton) lines in 1900.

The BRT leased the Culver line (formerly the Prospect Park & Coney Island Railroad) from the Long Island Railroad in 1899, and leased the Canarsie Railroad in 1906. This completed the Brooklyn Rapid Transit system that combined the Elevated Railroads with the former steam railroads to the shore. This all changed when the BMT leased the new Municipal Subway Lines built by the City of New York. This was contract No. 4 of the so-called Dual Contracts. After the BRT bankruptcy due to the disasterous Malbone Street wreck in 1918, the Brooklyn Manhattan Transit operated all the former BRT lines until June 1, 1940, when the City of New York took over the operation of all subway and elevated lines.

The new Lexington Avenue line is not yet open in this 1885 shot. A guard watches over the deck roof steam coaches with Brooklyn elevated railroad on their herald boards.

The new Park Avenue elevated of the Brooklyn Elevated Railroad had no ground connections to deliver the coaches or the locomotives, so a temporary ramp was built at Park Avenue and Grand Avenue. The equipment was hauled by car float to the Wallabout Market Dock then hauled over Brooklyn City tracks to the ramp. Locomotive Number One, The Seth Low and the first coaches with deck roofs are already in position. Loco Number 19 is about to climb to its elevated life of hauling Brooklynites.

A Fulton Street steam local train moves past Boro Hall in 1900 and it doesn't seem to disturb the population of the time at all. From baby carriages to horse drawn carriages, it's just part of the busy life of Brooklyn. The first coach is still lettered Kings County while the second (314) is lettered BRT. Later in time 314 will become 755 and pull its own train without puffing billy.

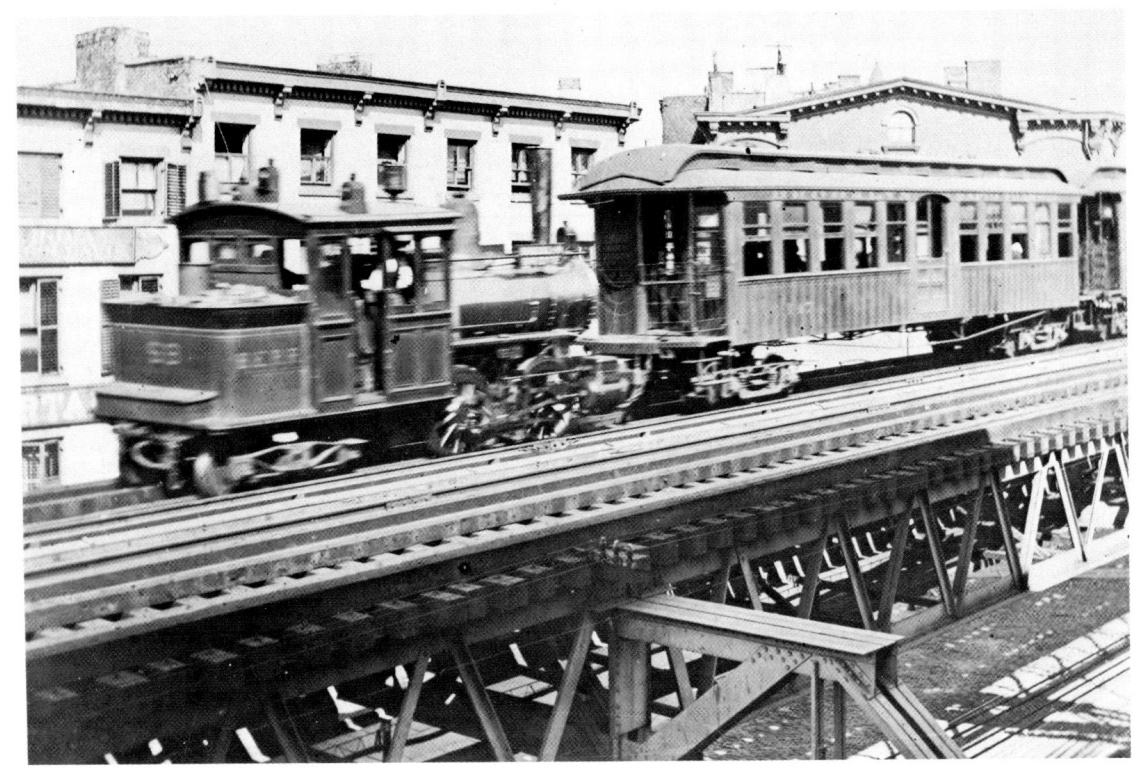

(far left) Number 53 travels down the Fulton El at South Oxford Street in 1901. (bottom) A cow catcher for an elevated locomotive was needed for the times they ran on the ground. Number 63 has one, some engines do not. On the roof of the cab, markers are used to indicate just what route they are. The photo was taken at East New York in 1901. (lower left) In 1894 to 1896, the Knights of Pythias ran specials from Cypress Hills to Ulmer Park. Number 70, a Rhode Island graduate class of 1888, leads the special train.

(top left) Number 11 has just been in service for one year when it is pictured at East New York. The forney was built by Rhode Island in 1885. The engine had 42" drivers and 11x16 cylinders. *(upper right)* Built in 1893 by Rhode Island the destination signs were hung on the boiler railing. These late comers have a number of lines to run on, for the system has really grown by this time. *(lower right)* Headed for the Queens border, City Line on the Fulton El, Number 28 is operating tender first, which is part of the forney engine's design.

Left:
From this photo you can see that steam is nearing the end of its day, because if you notice, the roof of the coach already has cat walks for trolley pole mounts.

(Top)
The building of the elevated required some of the telegraph lines to be raised, the air above Boro Hall will be darkened for a number of winters to come. The roof has not been applied to the Myrtle Avenue Station.

(Top Right)
It has been eight years since number one opened up Brooklyn to the era of steam elevated railroading.

(Bottom Right)
Engine 56 was side swiped and the towers switch rods held her on the structure. Tillary street station was cut in two for the Fulton line lead to the bridge yard. We see the station and walk over on September 6, 1900. The station will be closed and taken down.

(Upper left) Broadway Ferry area in 1890. A train bound for the ferry terminal has stopped at Driggs Street station next to the Williamsburg Savings Bank that still stands today. (Rigth) The Broadway Ferry station had two levels, but only the top ever had tracks. The Bridge could have ended any hopes of additional needs. The entrance to the Roosevelt Ferry can be seen. The opening of the Williamsburg Bridge will stop the ferry service and Broadway Ferry El service was reduced to a shuttle service to Marcy Avenue. Car 998 ran as a shuttle car on that service.

No. 3 (Top) pulls into Flatbush Avenue, the Fifth Avenue Line that crosses underneath has been painted out by the photographer. (Upper right) Engine No. 1 is at the rear of the Union Depot at Fifth Avenue and 36th Street on the Culver line. The trolley is on the West End line at the extreme right. The BRT operated over the L.I.R.R. to get to the Rockaways. In this 1901 view, we see No. 71 and in the rear, 3 an Ocean Electric car that shared part of the line with a Long Island train on the right. The crowds were so great that a line of trains and trolleys would stretch over the entire bay. Today the IND Rockaway line runs here. The joint BRT-LIRR operation to the Rock- aways ended after the summer of 1917 by order of the United States Railroad Administration.

TRAILERS TO MOTORS

A 1930 view of Car 17 as an electric trailer. Compare this car to the same series of original Brooklyn steam coaches on Page 22 and you can appreciate the amount of rebuilding the BRT put into its trailer fleet. This craftmenship enable number 17 to operate for another twenty years of service.

With electrification and unification of the elevated companies, the new BRT Company, through its chief engineer R. C. Taylor, designed the standards to convert steam coaches to motor cars or electric trailers. The changes made were the following —Enlarged and reenforced platforms, Van Dorn couplers and draft gear, new brake rigging, older trucks were reconstructed or Peckham Trucks (the BRT standard) were applied. (Upper Right) East New York shown with steam trailer and electric 500 series cars. (Bottom) Front end view of trailer 120 shows all the modification applied to all cars. (Bottom right) Car 120 interior shows the addition of electric lights, heaters and the famous straps for standees.

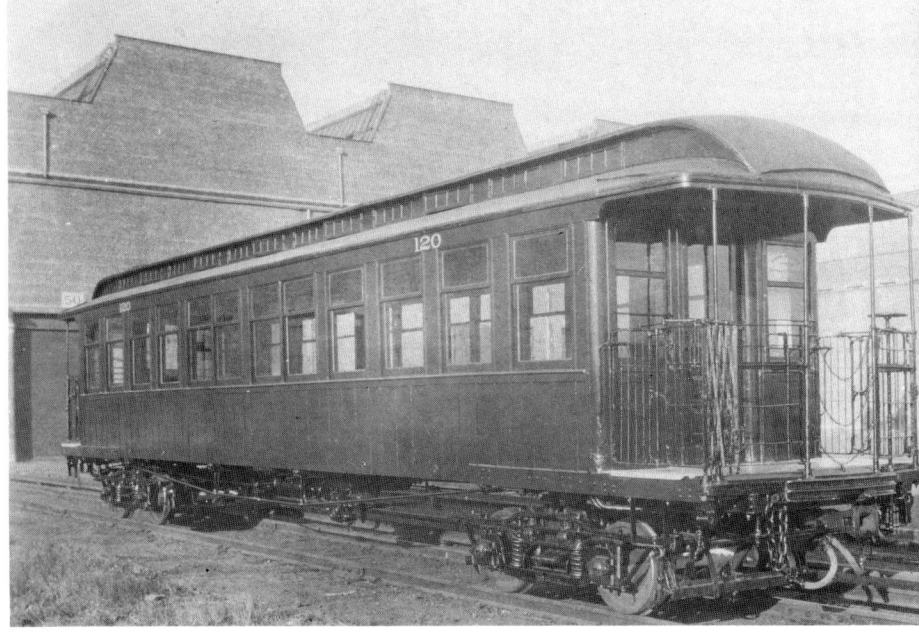

(Opposite Page Top) A Fifth Avenue train stopped at Ashland Place station. The El is supported so that work can continue on the new subway. The rebuilding of trailers enabled them to take the constant buffetting of their motorized sisters. (Opposite Page Bottom Left) 93 at Bay Parkway working a West End shuttle service. An early shot of 93 can be seen on Page 24 behind loco number 53. The car was renumbered from 142 shown. (Opposite Page Bottom) In 1930, car 120 is owned by New York Rapid Transit, the elevated division of the BMT. (Top) Manhattan seating plan of car 234 was popular on both sides of the East River. (Top Right) Car 234 is a trailer that did not receive a center door as did other of her type. Pictured at Fresh Pond in 1941. (Right) Soon No.3 will be bumped from the Flushing Line by the newly rebuilt Q's. The year is 1939 at Fiske Avenue.

(Left) The photograph shows the first electric elevated car order for Brooklyn. 400 is pictured in the Brooklyn Bridge yard on July 11, 1898. 400 has the controller mounted on the open platform like the New York and Brooklyn Bridge cable cars (See Page 18). (Lower Left) 410 was built by the Pullman Palace Car Company with McGuire Trucks and 4, 80HP Walker Motors. The electrical equipment was installed by the Brooklyn Elevated Railroad Company (Below). Car 400 will be rebuilt and renumbered over the years, and will finally emerge as Car 620, pictured here in 1941. 620 will end her service life for Brooklyn in 1951. If you compare the two photographs, you can estimate the many changes that have taken place over 50 years of service.

Cars 500-540 were built by Wason in 1898 (top). An Early shot running on the Fulton El with the cab on the platform and small markers on the roof (bottom) a front view shows that the motorman's door was opened by the conductor the same way the gates are operated. This was so they could operate with gate cars in a train. The whistle is on the roof, later when the controller was moved to the interior of the car, the whistle was moved over the motorman's window. 900 & 929 are the final rebuilt look of the 500s. Here the two cars are turning on to Myrtle Avenue at Grand Street in 1936. All trailers and motor cars were rebuilt to the BRT standards at 39th Street shops.

(Top) 755 at Coney Island in 1939. Ex-Kings County cars when rebuilt as motor cars have an extra steel support running under the center of the car. (Top Right) 669 at 36 Street shops in an Ex 450-499 motor car. (Right) 910 uses a small wood base to support its market lights on the roof. This series car has the clear-story vent window open on the ends. (Bottom) 602 and 760 are examples of same type steam coach with two different looks. 602 at Knickerbocker Avenue (note express track in service) is a motor without center door added, while 760 had a center door added as a steam coach. When motorized, the need for the center door ended. When ground operation ended, steps, trolley poles and headlights were removed from the roofs.

FOURTEEN
CAR SHIPMENT
(OF 50 CAR ORDER) MADE BY
THE JEWETT CAR CO., NEWARK, O.,
DEC. 19TH, 1901 TO BROOKLYN RAPID TRANSIT
CO. BROOKLYN, N.Y.

(Top left) 805 as a fully rebuilt motor car in 1905 (Top right) Interior of 759 showing how center doors no longer used were covered by seating (Center left) #450-499 order being delivered from Jewett in 1901 (Top) 617 at East New York yard in 1930 (Bottom left) 600 at 36th Street yard in 1930.

In the beginning of the morning rush car 27 of the Manhattan Bridge Three Cent line, is at the end of her run at Fulton Street and Flatbush Avenue extension. With the abandoning of the Manhattan Bridge service, they were purchased by the Queensborough Bridge Railway. A rush hour six car Fulton train above and a fairly new 8000 series Peter Witt turns on to Fulton. If you look you can see the blur of a Fifth Avenue train.

As this three car train in the bridge yard moves toward Sands Street, we get a good view of the bridge tower in the background. Semaphore signals are still used in this 1935 view.

Car 624 is the last car in this duo headed for 36th Street. Behind we can see the famous Brooklyn Fox, one of the five fabulous Fox theaters built across the country. A large number of film palaces attracted many Saturday night dates to take the El to them. The photograph was taken in 1940.

734 in Fresh Pond yard near the end of her career.

This early photograph shows the first car to be rebuilt with a center door for joint service with the N.Y. & Brooklyn Bridge Railway. The center door was used only at Park Row. 106 will also be equipped with a cable grip for travel over the bridge. This is before electrification of the Bridge road.

It is the midst of World War II but it is a quiet Sunday in Brooklyn and 754 and 104 rest on the express track on the West End line at 20th Avenue.

702 on the Broadway El will soon turn on Lexington for her trip to Sands Street in 1934.

754 along with trailer 217 will no more go a-roving over the roofs of Brooklyn.

(Above) Motor Car 439 at Brill Plant in 1900. (Above Right) What 439 and her sisters would finally look like in the form of 937. (Left) Interior of 937. (Lower Left) This trio of cars 920, 620 and 671, is at East New York headed for Eastern Parkway Station on the Broadway El.

Fresh Pond yard was home to open platform equipment till 1958.

White paint on the platform end of 661 means she is equipped with subway-type third rail shoes.

A group of center door BU's layover in East New York yard. Note fire wall used to separate wood equipment in case of fire.

926 is a work motor with yellow ends to prove it. 926 is a former 600 series car.

1000's 1100's CONVERTIBLES

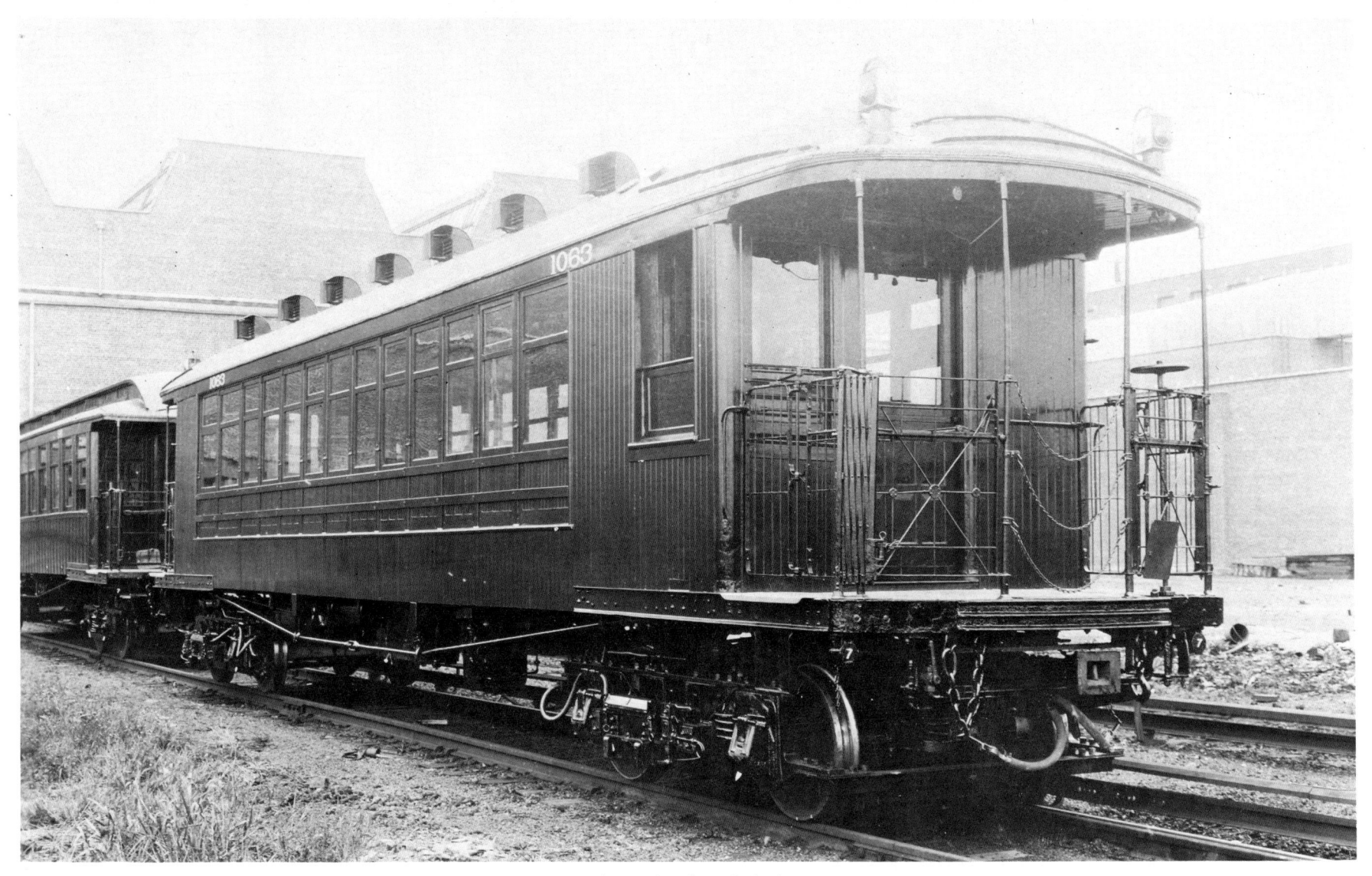

With their arch roofs, the 1000s were distinctive. The roof ends and platforms were more rounded then the other BUs that were built after them. They were the last cars built with split gates, cars 1200-1499 had Pitt Gates.)

Above
The builder wanted to show just how convertible a 1000 was. The seats are yet to be installed. The 1000s were the last to have a cabinet behind the cab for the controller. Later cars would use turret controllers.

Above Right:
1000s were the mainstay of the summer business. Here a 1000 turns on Bath Avenue, with a BRT trolley wrecker on the left.

Left:
It is the end of the season at Culver depot in 1915.

Left:
The panels are in and some are equipt with small windows that open. The 1000 had wood slat seats and a very plain arch roof that did not cool as well as a clearstory roof. The 1000 were the only non-railroad roof cars.

45

In 1936, 1044 leaves 36th Street Station headed for Third Avenue. The single car will have the conductor collect fares with a Johnson fare box mounted on the platform. Today the Brooklyn-Queens Expressway shadows the same space.

Another view showing a lone 1000 headed up the hill to Fifth Avenue. Number 5 of the South Brooklyn Railway heads some freight cars to the car floats.

What a wonderful transportation picture could be seen on Flatbush Avenue in 1935. When the Fouth Avenue subway was opened, the Fifth Avenue El never recovered from the loss of traffic.

1100 in the summer of 42 at Gates Avenue on the Broadway line.

A three car Culver train leaves 36th Street Station while a single 1000 on the Bay Ridge shuttle will soon enter the station for the trip to 65th Street.

47

1200's   1400's

New at the Brill plant. 1235 (left) show the elegant paint job the BRT ordered. The original idea for the 1200s was that they were semi-convertibles like the street cars. The windows could be removed and shades were the rider's only protection. The cars later only used open and windows and roof vents. The BRT put the poles, marker lights and other fittings on in their own shops.

1200 & 1400 (right top) had the same appearance, inside and out. The interior is the Manhattan type seating with cane seats. In the City ownership period the rear windows were covered by advertising racks. The 1200 & 1400s had a very handsome empire type roof.

1257 and 1438 (lower left & right) in a similiar pose for the company show you how exact the two series are to each other. Many of these cars became the mainstay of the C and Q types. Examples of both have been saved.

These cars had steel underframes, hence no turnbuckles. They were built for joint operation over the Long Island Rail Road to the Rockaways. They were designed to operate in trains with the all-steel L.I.R.R. MP41's.

Brighton Beach train emerging from the Eastern Parkway portal in 1914 (now the Franklin Shuttle).

The early years had a lot of surface running and most of the El cars had steps with trap doors for high level platforms. (lower) If this photograph were color we would get a good view of those red cars against the white snow in Fresh Pond yard. Note that it's all over head power in 1914. Fresh Pond yard would be the last haven for wood cars on the BMT. Ridgewood and Glendaleites would give directions. "You take the wood train to Bridge Street and the Steel train to Chambers Street."

51

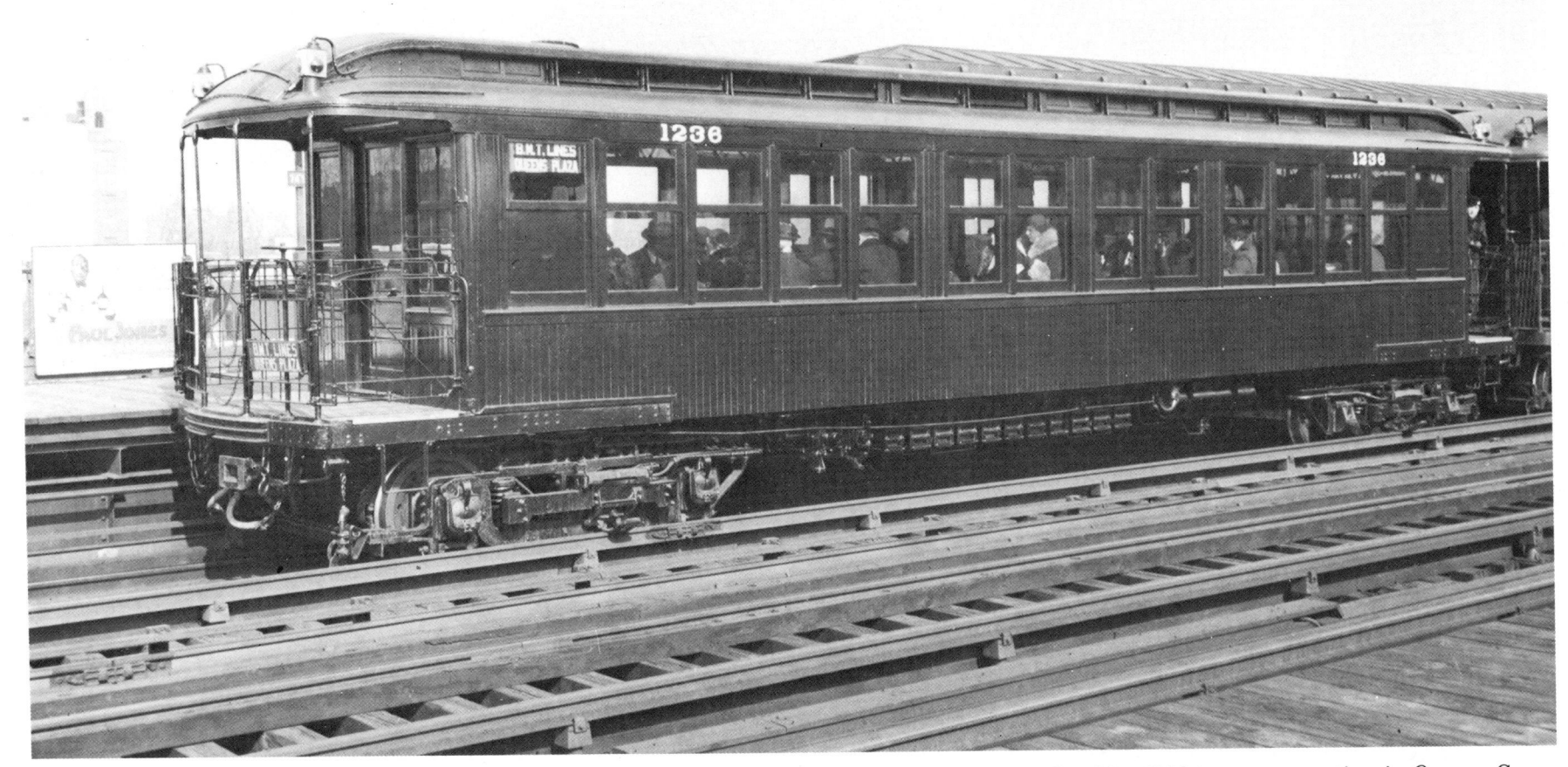

In 1935, 1236 is seen operating in Queens Service at 74th Street Station on the Flushing line. (Opposite Page) They were not only rebuilt into Qs, but unrebuilt back to BUs. Cars 1404, 1407, 1273, are now part of the Transit Museum Collection. The roofs were not rebuilt to the clearstory.

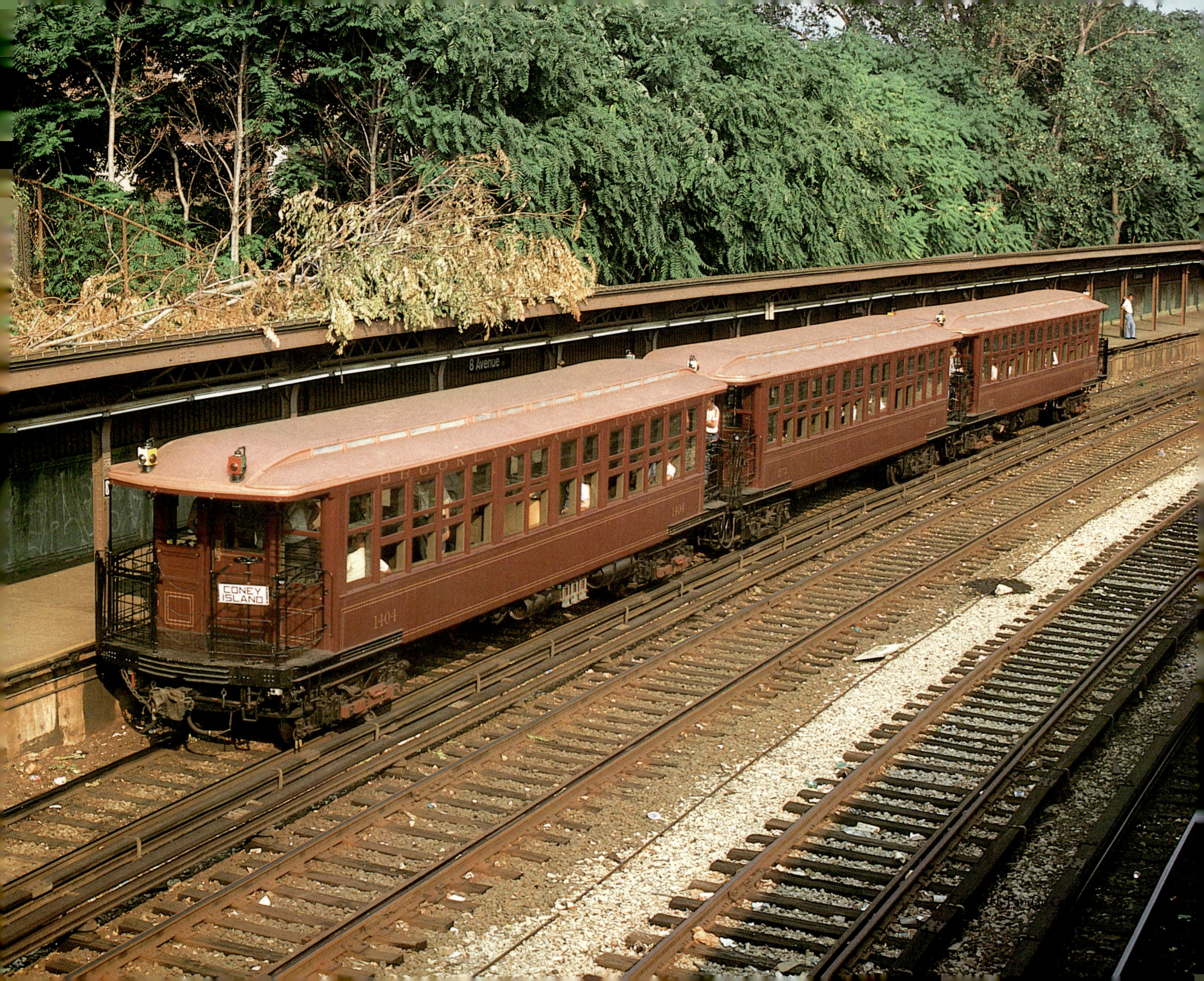
8 Avenue
CONEY ISLAND
1404

1300's
CONVERTIBLES

The 1300s were the last convertible gate cars built by the BRT. Part steel and wood the 1300s were built in an era where the BRT was thinking of subways. 1307 show the car with panels and 1312 with the panel out and bars in. Built by three builders, 1300 is seen lashed to a Cinncinati Car Company flat at the plant in 1905. The front of 1300 is seen later at 39th Street shops, where the poles and markers and other appointments were put on. Other El cars are being rebuilt in the background. The 1300s had flop over cane seats. The management affeared of winter put heaters under most seats but half were later taken out. On a cold winter night, the warm wood interior of a BU could not be matched for comfort. The 1300 series were the last open gate cars to run in North America.

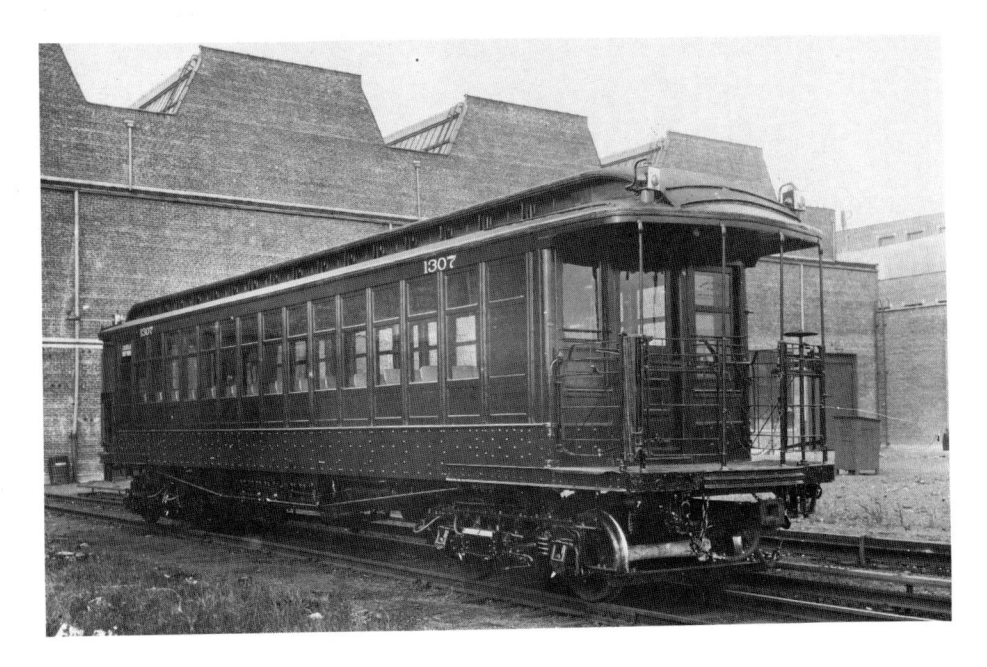

El cars never used a trolley retriever for the pole rope, they just tied them to the gates.

The white line on front platform signals this BU has subway type third rail shoes. It is Park Row just before the war. Later the structure will be used to help win the war.

The small kerosene lamps were used right to the end of the BU's operation. Fulton Ferry was closed as a station and used only as a cut back on the Fulton El.

When the city took over, these titles were written across the herald boards in the later years, it was not kept up. Car #1350 on Fulton Lexington line at Chauncey Street in 1943.

The Fulton El with 1317, 226 and 1375 leaving Crescent Street Station. As the years went on, fewer panels were removed until the end when only four panels were removed from each side.

This is how you remember the BUs, even with little maintenance they operated through a 1958 blizzard that crippled all the Southern and Eastern division except for the Myrtle Avenue El.

(Above Left)
For a day 1316 with signs to match went back in time as the Branford Trolley Museum fan trip celebrates the last days of BU operation.

On fan trips the faithful can visit haunts they only dream about. Coming off the Fulton Cut, the 5 car train winds around East New York Yard.

It must be really hot because a BU has its front door open "Its Hot." The Multi conductor has made himself cooler too. Multis had full cabs. The Bridge in the rear is The New York Connecting Railroad—New Haven Hill Gate Bridge route to Bay Ridge Brooklyn.

1307 and a partner in Fresh Pond yard. At night a 2 car BU would operate the Myrtle El with a conductor collecting fares on board. Many a quiet Brooklyn night was broken with the sound of working BUs.

Above:
A white flagged BU work train on the Fulton El making ready the end of Fulton service. The IND connection is being assembled to the left between Grant and Hudson Avenues.

Above Right:
An unused Staten Island Rapid Transit car was used as an office at the end of Fresh Pond yard until a few years later when a Q rammed into it. The old Trolley Conductor's Building is to the left and the trolley poles that once served the trolley yard and the El cars.

1326 with her trolley poles reversed as a work horse to haul flats and gondola cars with subway type couplers. Still in color we get an idea of what she would have looked like running on the ground for many a summer in the early part of the century.

REBUILT

1261 is not a 1200 series car. The BRT rebuilt from its fleet of steam coaches a number of replacement cars that were renumbered for cars that were wrecked, burned or whatever, in a series. Some of these cars were numbered in the 1000 series, then they were given 1200 and 1400 series cars that were being converted for the C & Q type cars.

1448 on a fan trip on the Lexington Avenue Line in 1949. The interior (Right) shows reverse seats, not the Manhattan seating plan of the true 1400 series. (Below) In 1923 the BMT rebuilt Cars 1498, 189, 1499, floors were re-enforced, and their hand gates replaced with pneumatically controlled gates. This was the BMT's response to the IRT's rebuilding of some of their gate cars to MUDC units. The test was not satisfactory and the BMT would go much further than the IRT with the appearance of the C type of which this trio will become C unit 1503.

The interior of 1448 shows she is not a true 1400.

"C" TYPE

In 1923, the new management of the BMT which organized the elevated lines under the New York Rapid Transit Company, started the experiments that would lead to the fleets of C type and Q type rebuilts. After the pneumatic gate cars, a second attempt was tried with cars 1496, 188 and 1497. They emerged as the first C type train. This first unit would be different from the other C types to come later. The front end (far left) was constructed of wood and was wider than the rest of the body, thus giving the end a puffed up appearance. This was to give the conductor a great view over the platform crowds. The train was also equipt with a PA system. Some Standard BMT subway cars also at this time experimented with PA systems. The brake wheel was on the outside of the car and all conductor's controls were inside. The roof ends remained untouched at both ends of the cars. The end platforms were just enclosed. The pneumatic doors were in the center of the car and slid into an outside pocket rather than into the car body itself. Gates protected the passage between cars. The interior in all three cars was longtitudinal seating. The units kept their elevated type third rail shoes. 1498, 189 and 1499 were next rebuilt to match the first set. In these years several ideas must have been in the mind of Mr. William Menden, the principal architect of the BMT fleet. For in 1925, 1502 and 1503 emerged with a different appearance. At the same time the BMT subway car "D" types were being delivered and there are similiarities in the look: Brutish and heavy. The second batch of C types had steel fronts that were body width and no PA systems. The pnuematic doors were moved toward either end but remained outside the body; that was easier to build but troublesome in bad weather. The trailer as a center car and the end of each motor car facing the center unit had these platforms removed and their roof cut straight with a drum type diaphram to connect the cars. The "D" cars were articulated and their drum connection was located over the truck being shared by each unit. With the C types the management did not go that far. The conductor's controls like the D types were located outside, but when running as a single unit, could be controlled from the inside. The two original units were rebuilt to look like the other 25 unit fleet, except for their center door design which stayed as it was. The C types were no beauty queens and they looked like nothing else anywhere.

63

(Top Left) Each B unit was re-enforced with steel girders under their floors. (Top) Two units leave Saratoga Avenue on the Fulton Street line. (Left) 1501 was made over to look like her sister C types with steel fronts. The center doors remained the same.

64

Almost a wooden version of the BMTs steel triplex units. 1511 at Coney Island shops in 1940. (Lower Right) 1519 is the last C type on the Fulton El ending a great era of transpoation. Trains will no longer run past Martin's, Nams & Loggers or Abraham & Strauss Department Stores. (Bottom Left) 1501 on the last day of Fulton Street service below Rockaway Avenue station.

Atlantic Avenue station on Fulton El, near the end of servi

Rockaway Station with the center platform made of wood was a later addition. When the line was cut back to Rockaway Avenue, the wood center platform was built over the express track and the old steel station was unused.

Fulton El was left in its original form along Pitken Avenue. The only subway cars that could use the light structure were the 1936 Multi's.

Fulton trains on the weekend terminated on the Broadway line at Eastern Parkway. The East New York El network is the most complex in the system.

Not very handsome, but hard workers until the very end. Our more advanced steel equipment, far more refined, unfortunately doesn't seem to hold up so well or as long.

"Q" TYPE

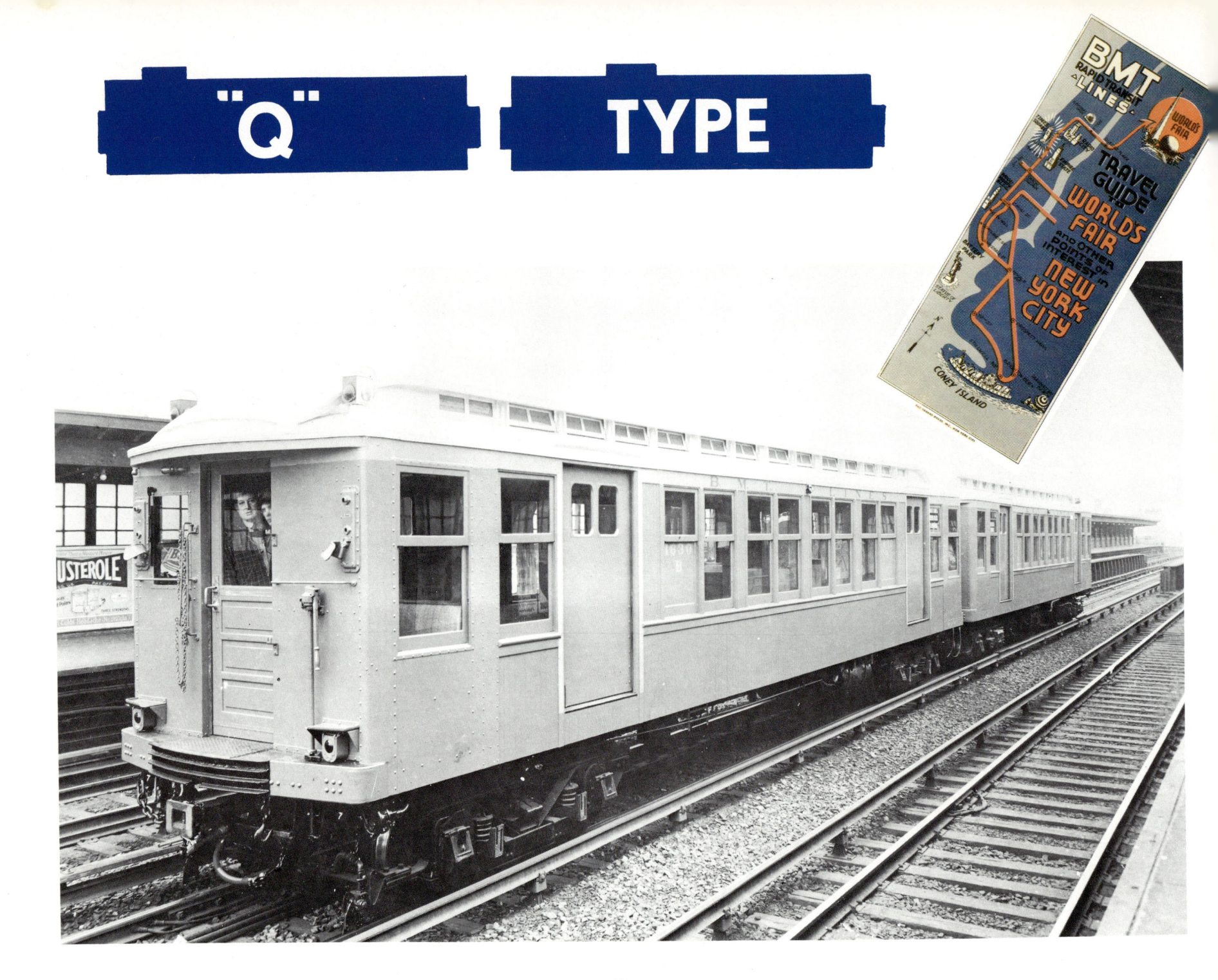

The Qs were the last rebuilding of wood elevated equipment undertaken by the BMT management. The Qs standing for Queens the borough, had perhaps the most interesting career of all the El cars in Brooklyn. In 1939, a great event in New York history happened with the Worlds Fair in Flushing Meadows, Queens. The management decided to rebuild 90 1200 and 1400 series cars into three car units with closed platforms and pnuematic doors. The IRT ordered new cars for the service using trucks from their older cars. The Qs differed from the C types, with the doors built too close into the car body. The roof line was not changed. The Qs did not have the wide bottom skirting the C types had to use to meet the 10 foot platform designed for subway cars, the Qs only had a step. The middle unit was made into a trailer and simple chains connected the cars. All door controls were the same as the C type units. From the start, the units got the fancy color scheme of blue and orange—the city's and the fair's colors, with BMT LINES painted on their herald boards. In 1939-1940, 13 two car units called QXs were buiilt for the World's Fair service. (left) New QX 1630 on the Flushing express track. The interior photograph is that of 1640 with many ads for World's Fair events. The Qs kept the Manhattan style seating plan. The front view is that of the first Q type, 1600A. Each unit carried the same number with the addition of A, B or C unit. They ran on the Flushing line until 1949 when they were bumped from the service and stored at the Avenue X yards of the Coney Island shops. That same year units 1680 and 1615 along with single unit 1634A were sent to the IRT's 241 Street shops to test seven car express trains on the Third Avenue El. The experiment was a success but the heavier BU trucks were replaced with the trucks of the scrapped composite cars that the Qs were replacing. In 1950, 1600-1629 were sent to the Bronx after being refurbished. The marker lights were moved to the center of the roof to clear Third Avenue stations along the line. The Qs gave good service till the end of the Third Avenue El in Manhattan. Again the Qs returned to Coney Island. Other Qs were used on the BMT in work service and on the South Brooklyn Railway were they received trolley poles. In 1958 the Transit Authority decided to replace the 1300 series convertibles on the Myrtle El, thus ending the era that started with the first El lines. Again the Qs were refurbished. Painted deep Maroon with light gray roofs, they started appearing in the Fresh Pond yards. Because of their composite trucks, they were very slow and could just make the grade to Broadway. The 1300 series trucks were not used to replace the composite trucks. The Qs served the Myrtle El until the TA finally "speeded up" transportation along Myrtle Avenue by tearing down the El, replacing it with the Myrtle Avenue bus. The last point to point El was gone as a fast link to downtown. The El's disappearance did little to enhance the area and made travel much more tiresome and lengthy. The Qs brought down the curtain of wood equipment in the system.

69

70

Opposite Page (Top Left) 1610 A, B, & C when new, at Lowery Street station with an orange body and blue trim. Some Qs had blue bodies with orange trim. Opposite Page (Top Right) D type 6058 and an unnumbered Q type pose to show off their new paint jobs. The D type is painted deep brown with a silver roof. Opposite Page (Bottom Left) 1600 at Queensborough Plaza with a blue body and orange trim. The Queens lines were host to the BUs of the BMT and the gate cars of the IRT Second Avenue El. Opposite Page (Bottom Right) QX 1640 A&B ex 1440 & 1204, new at Flushing Yards. (Lower Left) The northern side of Queensborough Plaza Station with the Qs running on the Astoria line in 1949.

(Upper Right) Complete with knuckle couplers for freight shipment, 1619 and 1618 are pulled by a New Haven steeple cab electric at Oak Point Yard for delivery to the Third Avenue El in 1950. (Lower Right) The Qs have made the big time, here on Third Avenue and 45 Street Manhattan with 1606 as a downtown express.

LIPKIN'S

BOWERY DEPT STORE
Admiration Cigars
"MILD TO THE LAST INCH!"

1605
A

(Opposite Page Top Left) A Q Express crosses the Harlem River in the last year of service. (Opposite Page Left) Downtown express train of Q types will soon be level with a local train of MUDC cars. (Opposite Page Lower Left) 1621C coming into Canal Street station in 1955. (Opposite Page Right) 1605 on a weekend layup. Note IRT composite trucks and third rail shoes. (Top Left) stored Qs are being slowly refurbished at Coney Island shops in 1957. (Bottom) 1605 now a Fresh Pond yard. The track work in the foreground was attempt to convert Fresh Pond carbarn to an elevated shop. A new bus garage was built instead. (Bottom Right) The last design change was a design disaster, that of lowering the clear—story roof. Fans were added, but the open clearstory window vents worked better. 1600 makes the turn at Wyckoff Avenue Station in 1967.

73

After 25 year absence, 1622 pays her respect on the 1964 World Fair in the original BMT colors.

1622 some years later at the old Metropolitan Avenue Station being made of wood burned and was replaced by concrete.

QX 1635 working as a work horse on the Flushing line with lowered roof, low marker lights and knuckle couplers. The QX did not have the luck the 3 unit sisters had.

The elevated lines did their job well for the large expanse of downtown Brooklyn that came about because of the ability of transit lines to move people; that in later days has been forgotten.

The sun sets on a new role for the Qs but for those of us who loved the 1300 series BUs on Myrtle—they were the enemy.

WORK CARS

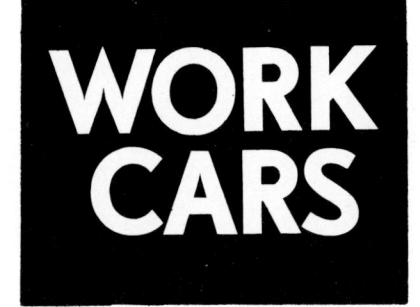

76

(left) Ex steam coach 26 now supply car 695 with an extra wide center door. (bottom far left) The money collection car picked up all the nickles for all the stations. (bottom left) 993 was another steam trailer rebuilt to a motorized work car. 993 gave the motorman his own door. (bottom) A model builder's darling is wrecker 3150. It was built with sister wrecker 3151 in 1904 by the company shops and used on the southern division with 3151 on the Eastern. (right) A number of surplus steam coaches were rebuilt for work service, like ex802 used as a supply car. They moved material from the store house at Coney Island shops to the other depots.

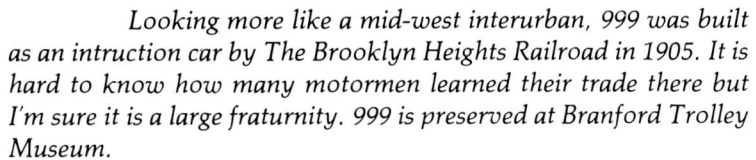

Looking more like a mid-west interurban, 999 was built as an intruction car by The Brooklyn Heights Railroad in 1905. It is hard to know how many motormen learned their trade there but I'm sure it is a large fraturnity. 999 is preserved at Branford Trolley Museum.

A number of high numbered 700s like 753 were used as snow sweepers with large brooms to clear the line.

996 was a work car assigned to East New York. The Trommer's Brewery neighbored the yard.

1642 a QX finished her days as a work motor for the South Brooklyn Railroad. The single car is equipped with subway couplers and trolley poles.

3060 is a King's County flat car used to transport sand to the stations.

BRT ELECTRIC LOCOMOTIVE

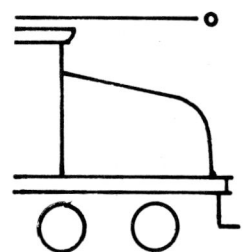

No. 1 was built by the BRT at the 39th Street Shop and is pictured there, brand new. No. 2 at Coney Island Shops gives a better view of the all wood body. In 1930, No. 2 wears BMT logo on her cab. (Bottom) No. 3 is a steel unit seen here pushing 4179 to its final stop. No. 4, the only box cab design locomotive on the system is busy doing track work at Stillwell Avenue. No. 5 is brand new on the American Locomotive turntable. No. 6 with poles, third rail shoes and dual couplers for subway and elevated cars, is lettered for New York Municipal Railway at 39th Street Yard in the late 20's. No. 5 is working South Brooklyn Railway freight at 39th Street Yard. Today, all subway and elevated work is performed by diesel engines.

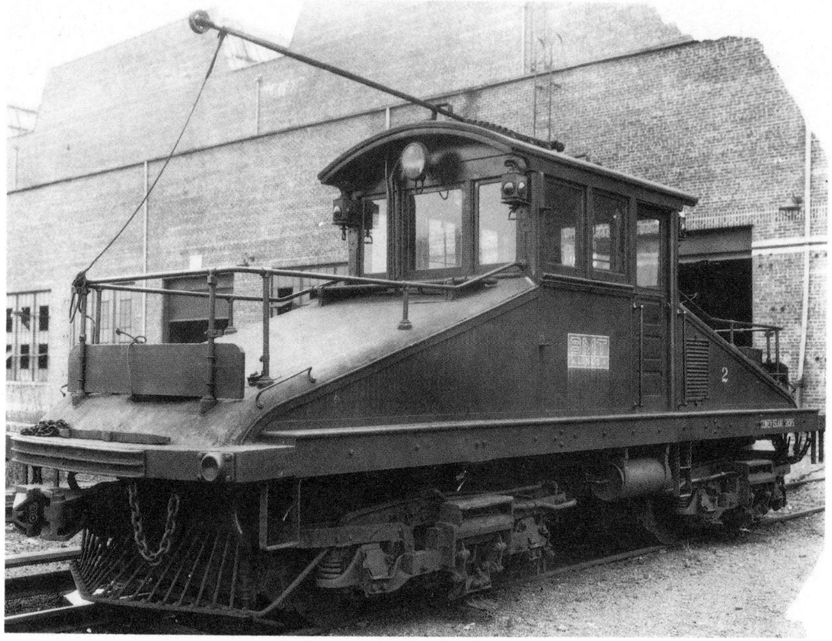

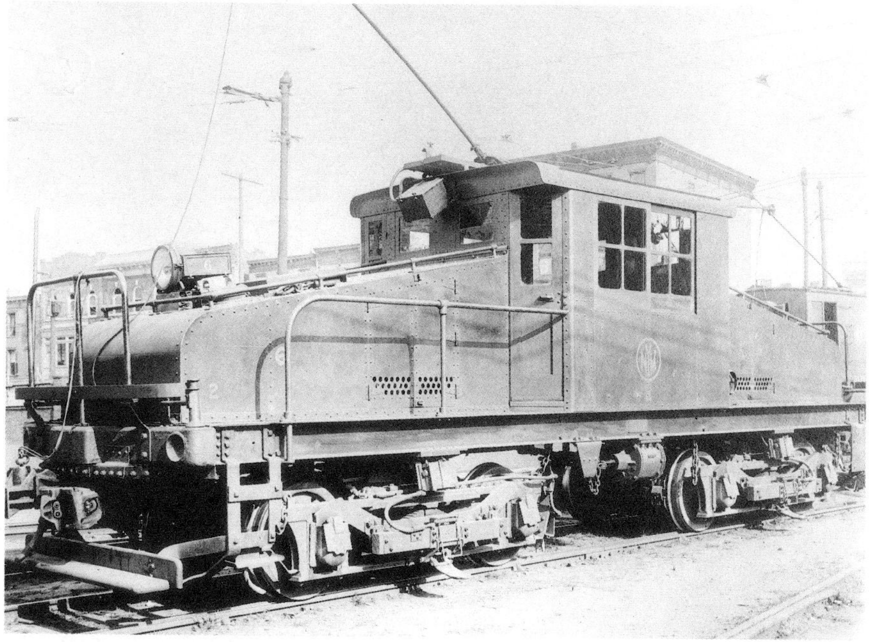

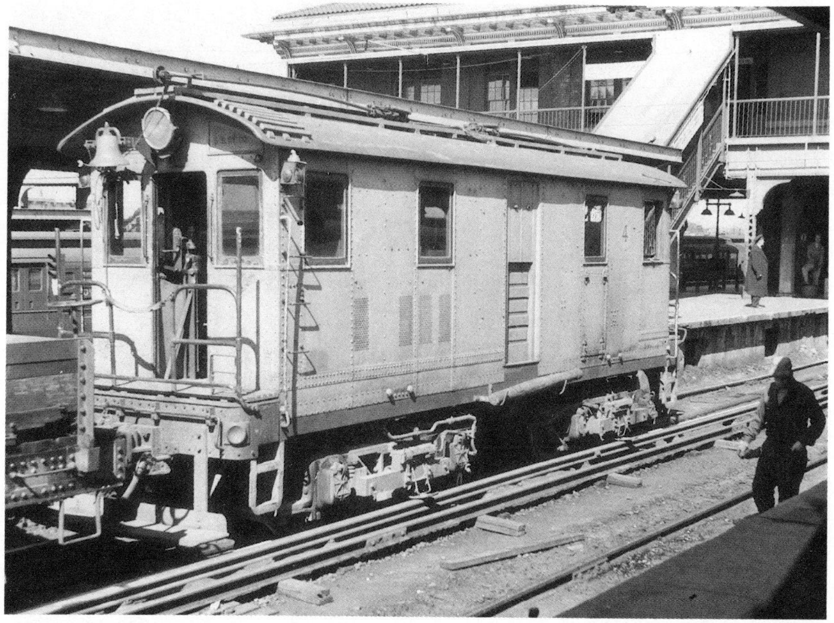

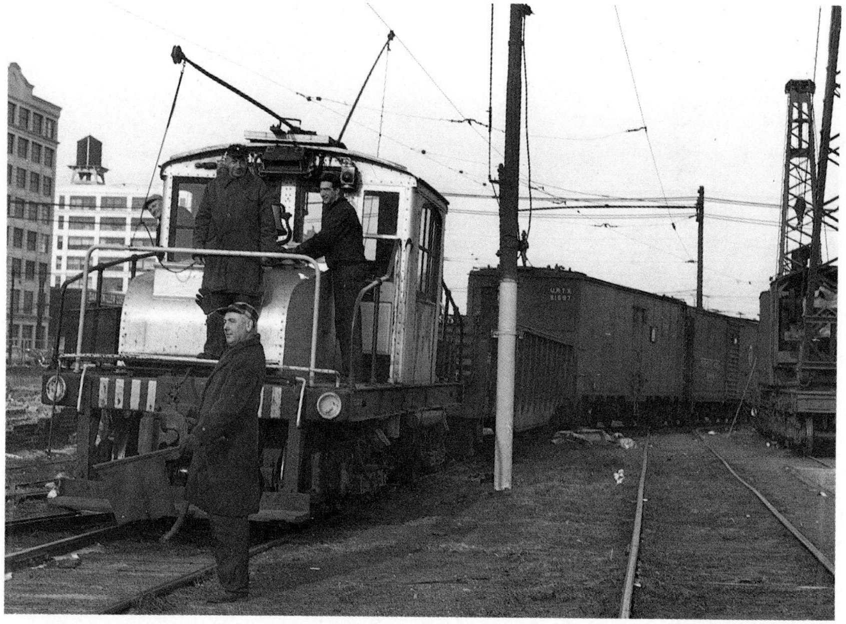

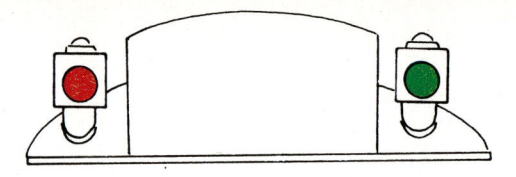

ROUTES AND MARKERS

Marker lights are to be adjusted by motormen to correspond with route on which train is running as follows:

ASTORIA-FLUSHING LINE

Queens Plaza to Flushing or Ditmars Avenue. —Both directions. ○ ○

Queens Plaza to 111th St. ○ ●(green)

Lay up trains on both branches. ●(yellow) ●(yellow)

BROADWAY LINE

Rockaway Parkway-Chambers St.—Both directions. ○ ●(yellow)

Rockaway Parkway-Canal Street—Both directions. ●(red) ○

Chambers Street or Canal Street to Eastern Parkway. Eastern Parkway or Atlantic Avenue to Canal Street. ●(green) ○

Chambers Street or Canal Street to Atlantic Avenue. Eastern Parkway or Atlantic Ave. to Chambers St. ○ ○

14th STREET-CANARSIE LINE

6th Avenue-Rockaway Parkway—Both directions. ●(red) ●(red)

Myrtle Ave.-6th Ave.—Both directions. ●(green) ●(green)

Atlantic Ave.-6th Ave.—Both directions. ●(red) ●(green)

CULVER LINE

Coney Island or Kings Highway-Park Row—Both directions. ●(yellow) ●(red)

Coney Island or Kings Highway-Sands Street—Both directions. ●(yellow) ○

9th Ave.-Kings Highway—Both directions. ●(green) ●(red)

MARKER LIGHTS

FIFTH AVE. LINE

65th Street-Sands Street—Both directions. ●(green) ●(green)

FULTON ST. LINE

Lefferts Avenue-Park Row—Both directions. ●(green) ●(green)

Grant Avenue-Park Row—Both directions. ●(red) ○

Lefferts Ave., Grant Ave. or Atlantic Ave., to King County Terminal. ●(green) ●(yellow)

Lefferts Ave., Grant Ave. or Atlantic Ave., to Fulton Ferry. ●(red) ●(green)

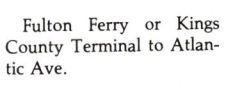

Fulton Ferry or Kings County Terminal to Atlantic Ave. ●(red) ●(green)

Fulton Ferry or Kings County Terminal to Lefferts Ave. ●(green) ●(yellow)

Fulton Ferry or Kings County Terminal to Grant Ave. ○ ●(green)

Atlantic Avenue-Park Row—Both directions. ●(yellow) ○

Kings County Terminal-Lefferts Ave.—Both directions. Express Franklin to Atlantic Ave. ○ ○

Franklin Ave.-Grant Ave.—Both directions (Sundays and holidays). ●(red) ●(red)

LEXINGTON AVE. LINE

168th St., 111th St., Crescent St., or Eastern Parkway-Sands St. Sands St.-168th St. ●(red) ○

Jamaica, 111th St., Crescent St. or Eastern Parkway-Park Row. Park Row-Eastern Parkway—Both directions. ●(red) ●(green)

168th St. (Jamaica)-Chambers St.—Both directions. ●(green) ●(green)

Park Row, Chambers Street or Canal Street-111th Street. ●(red) ●(red)

Park Row, Chambers Street or Canal Street-Crescent Street. ●(yellow) ●(green)

MYRTLE AVE. LINE

Metropolitan Avenue or Wyckoff Avenue to Sands Street. Park Row or Sands Street to Metropolitan Ave. ●(green) ○

Metropolitan Avenue or Wyckoff Avenue to Park Row. Park Row or Sands St. to Wyckoff Ave. ○ ○

Metropolitan Avenue-Chambers Street—Both directions. ●(red) ●(green)

Chambers Street to Kings Highway or Brighton Beach (Brighton Line). ●(red) ●(green)

Chambers Street-Fresh Pond Road—Both directions. ●(red) ○

ALL LINES

Shop or Lay-up Train. ●(yellow) ●(yellow)

82

B. M. T. SERVICE TO WORLD'S FAIR

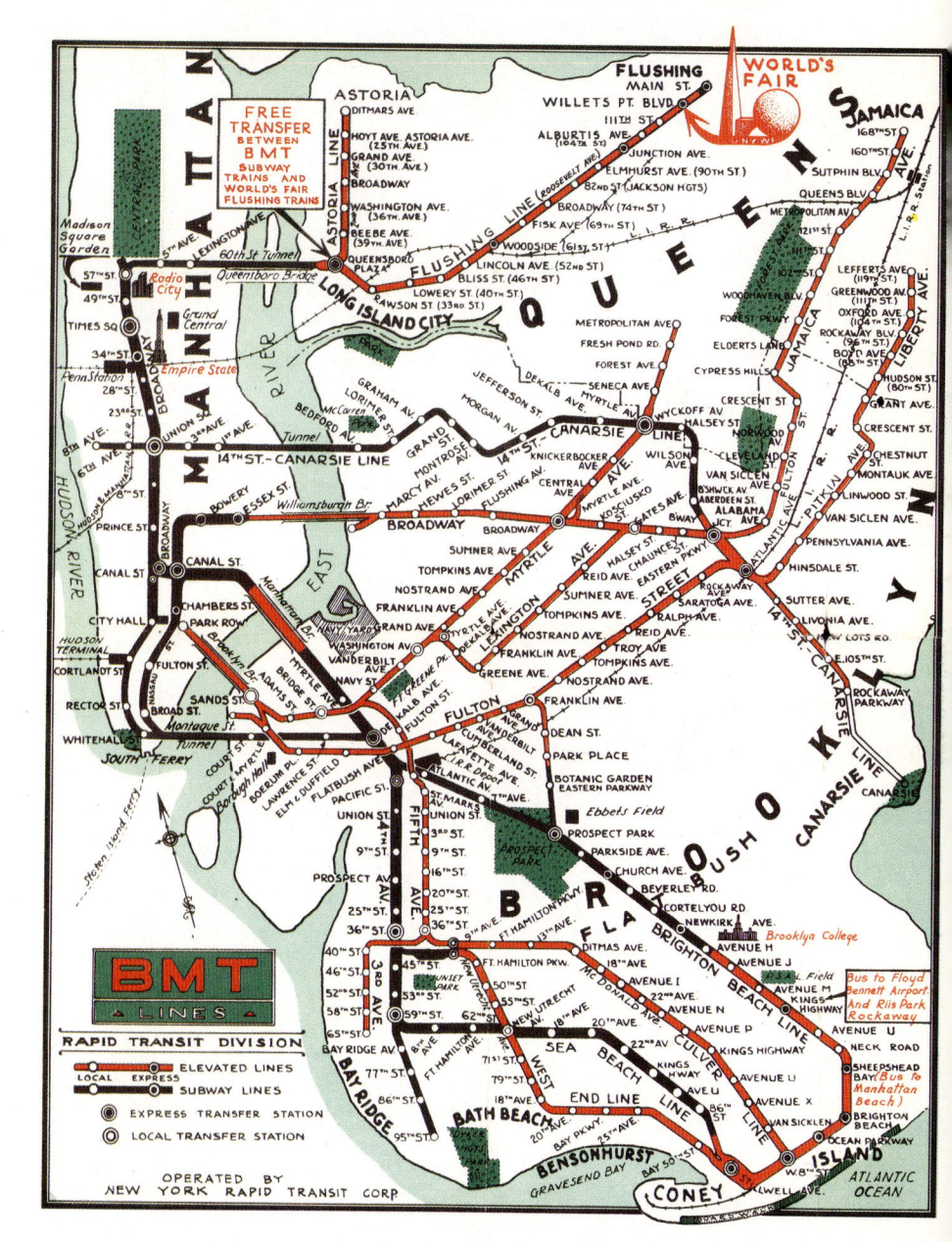

TIME POINTS AND NORMAL RUNNING TIME

ASTORIA-FLUSHING LINE

Queens Plaza to Main St., Flushing	21
Queens Plaza to Ditmars Ave., Astoria	8

BROADWAY "L" LINE

Rockaway Parkway to Atlantic Ave.	8
Atlantic Ave. to Marcy Ave.	18
Marcy Ave. to Chambers St.	10
Total	36

BROADWAY-JAMAICA

	Local	Express
168th St. to 111th St.	9	9
111th St. to Eastern Parkway	18	18
Eastern Park'y to Myrtle Ave.	9	5
Myrtle Ave. to Marcy Ave.	6	3
Marcy Ave. to Chambers St.	10	10
Total	52	45

Express trains operate over middle track in Broadway between Eastern Parkway and Marcy Ave., except express trains leaving Jamaica 6.06 A.M. and Chambers St. 3.09 P.M. to 4.58 P.M. use express tracks between Myrtle Ave. and Marcy Ave.

CULVER LINE

	Local	Express
Stillwell Ave. to Kings High'y	9	9
Kings Highway to 9th Ave.	14	16
9th Ave. to Navy St.	17	14
Navy St. to Park Row	10	10
Total	50	49

Express trains make no station stops between 36th St., and 9th St., and Atlantic Ave., East and West bound in the A.M. rush. East bound only in the P.M. rush.

FIFTH-AVE.-BAY RIDGE

65th St. to 36th St.	7
36th St. to Sands St. (Loop)	19
Total	26

FULTON ST. LINE

	Local	Express
Lefferts Ave. to Grant Ave.	9	9
Grant Ave. to Atlantic Ave.	10	13
Atlantic Ave. to Franklin Ave.	13	7
Franklin Ave. to Sands St.	12	12
Sands St. to Park Row	5	5
Total	49	46

Express trains use middle track in Fulton St. between Atlantic Ave. and Nostrand Ave.

LEXINGTON AVE. LINE

111th St. to Crescent St.	9
Crescent St. to Eastern Parkway	9
Eastern Parkway to Myrtle Ave.	17
Myrtle Ave. to Park Row	14
Total	49

MYRTLE AVENUE

Metropolitan Ave. to Wyckoff Ave.	6
Wyckoff Ave. to Grand Ave.	12
Grand Ave. to Sands St.	9
Sands St. to Park Row	5
Total	32

MYRTLE AVE.-CHAMBERS ST.

	Local	Express
Metropolitan Ave. to Broadway	12	13
Broadway to Chambers St.	16	13
Total	28	26

Express trains operate over middle track, between Myrtle Ave. and Marcy Ave.

14TH ST.-CANARSIE LINE

	Local	Express
Rockaway Park'y to Atl. Ave.	8	9
Atlantic Ave. to Myrtle Ave.	7	8
Myrtle Ave. to Lorimer St.	11	9
Lorimer St. to 6th Ave.	9	9
Total	35	35

RATES OF PAY

AGREEMENT made this 23rd day of July, 1929, between the herein named classes of employees of Group B of New York Rapid Transit Corporation and New York Rapid Transit Corporation, governing the rates of pay, rules and working conditions effective August 3, 1929.

CONDUCTORS

Per Hour
- Grade "A"— Third year of service and thereafter .... 60 cents
- Grade "B"—First two years of service .... 59 cents
- Freight service only .... 66 cents

TRAINMEN

- Grade "A"— Fifth year of service and thereafter .... 56 cents
- Grade "B"— Third and Fourth year of service .... 55 cents
- Grade "C"— Second year of service .... 53 cents
- Grade "D"— First year of service .... 52 cents

1880-1920

The forty years from 1880 to 1920 bore witness to the construction and reconstruction of the Brooklyn Elevated network, the integration of the Brooklyn steam excursion railroads and street car lines with the elevated lines and their electrification. The period included the organization of grade crossing commissions to fund and oversee the reconstruction of a number of the early steam excursion railroads, most notably the Brighton Beach, which became the world's first four track, high speed electric railroad. It was the model for many similar projects throughout the world, including the London to Brighton main line of the Southern (London, Brighton & South Coast) Railway.

Three bridges; Brooklyn, Manhattan and Williamsburgh, were constructed to carry Brooklyn elevated trains between the Boroughs of Brooklyn and Manhattan. The Dual Contracts were signed by the City of New York with the Interborough Rapid Transit Company (Contract No. 3) and New York Municipal Railway Corporation (Contract No. 4); the latter an affiliate of the BMT. Under Contract 4, the City built new subway and elevated lines and strengthened some of the original Brooklyn elevated lines so that a new, integrated subway-elevated network was inaugurated serving Brooklyn, Manhattan and Queens.

All of this construction was in place by 1920; four decades before the terms Pre-metro and light rail transit were invented to describe what by comparison are very modest projects. By 1920, the Brooklyn subway-elevated network was already carrying nearly one billion passengers annually!

The maps used on these pages are the original BRT drawings showing the system's original layout before contract four construction drastically changed the system, much as it looks today.

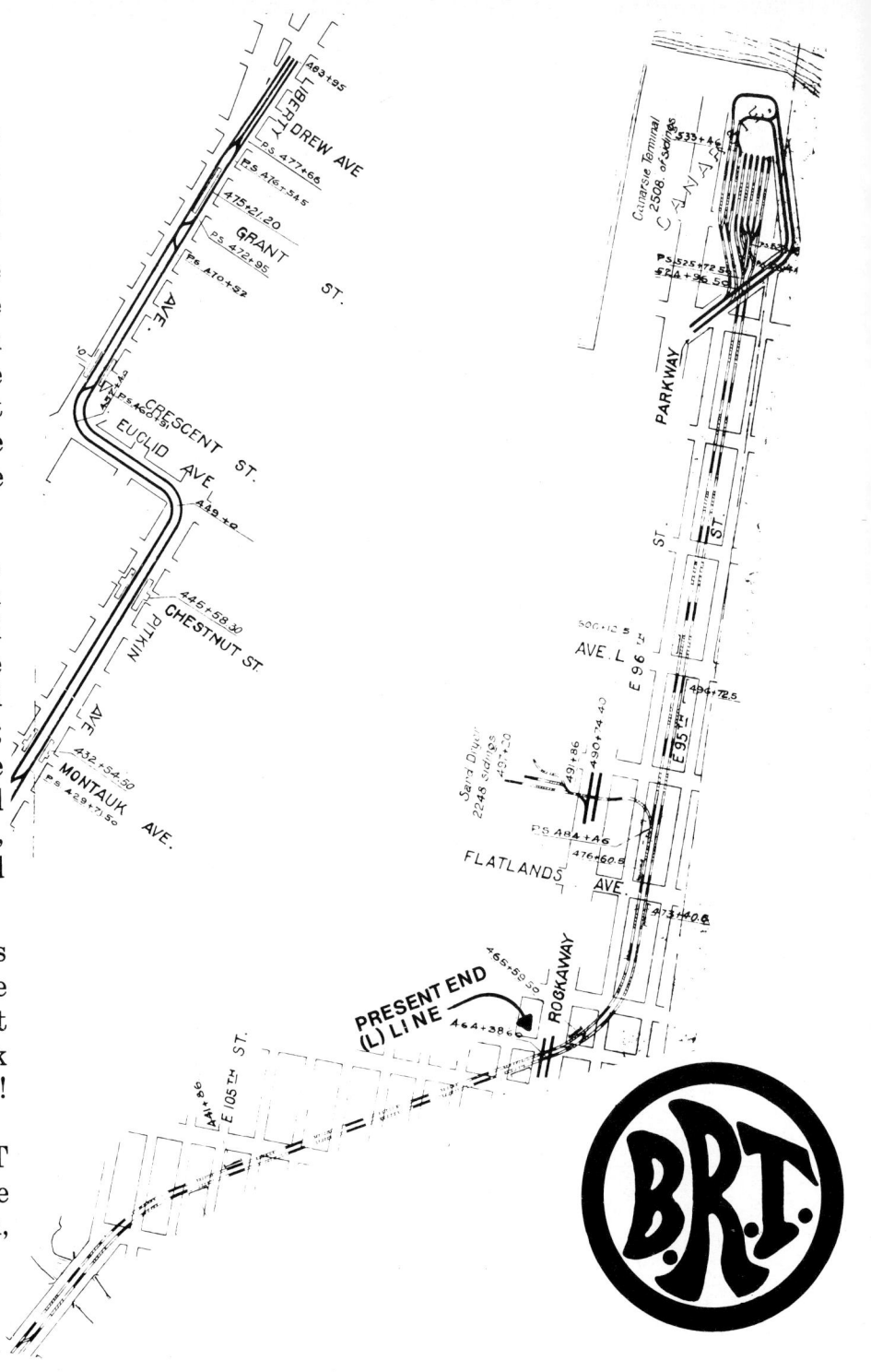

Right:
The Canarsie Terminal in 1915 was a busy place and from the surroundings, one can see why. Later a trolley shuttle replaced the El terminal with a simple loop, but leaving most of the yard. Today the Belt Parkway crosses the area.

Below Rigth:
The only grade crossing on the system was at 105th Street on the Canarsie line which lasted until the 1970's. A Multi Section in light tan color scheme moves across into 105th Street Station.

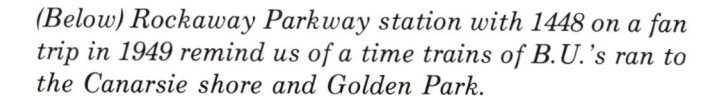

(Below) Rockaway Parkway station with 1448 on a fan trip in 1949 remind us of a time trains of B.U.'s ran to the Canarsie shore and Golden Park.

85

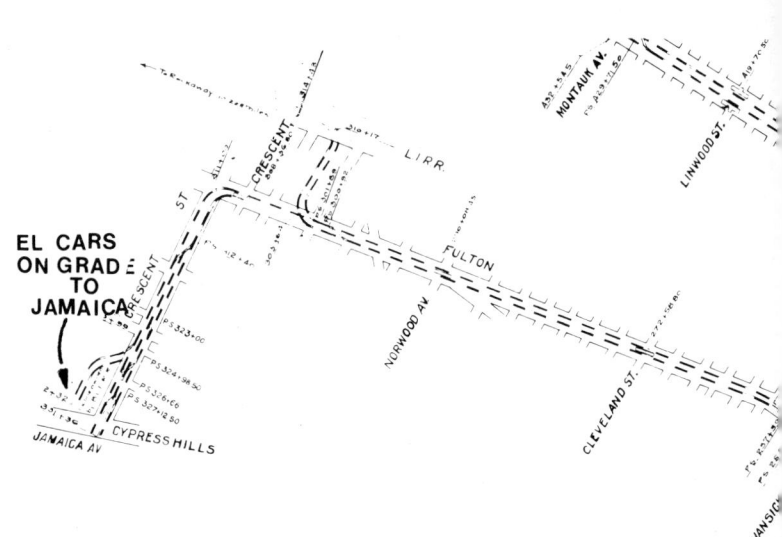

Fulton Street with BUs 701 and 601 headed into Alabama Avenue Station. This is a busy area in 1906 with 2 hotels, at least 3 saloons and a theater in the picture. A lot of money came to these establishments from BRT men who worked at the East New York yard or the East New York car barn. The Muller Hotel still stands on the corner today.

Today East New York is one of the last great elevated yards and shops still functioning. Our first shot shows Manhattan Junction and tower in the back with a sea of 8 and 10 window streetcars. The second shot shows the right side and a sea of wood El cars. Each BRT yard had gardens and with stones proudly spelling out its name. In the far right is locomotive number one in these 1916 shots.

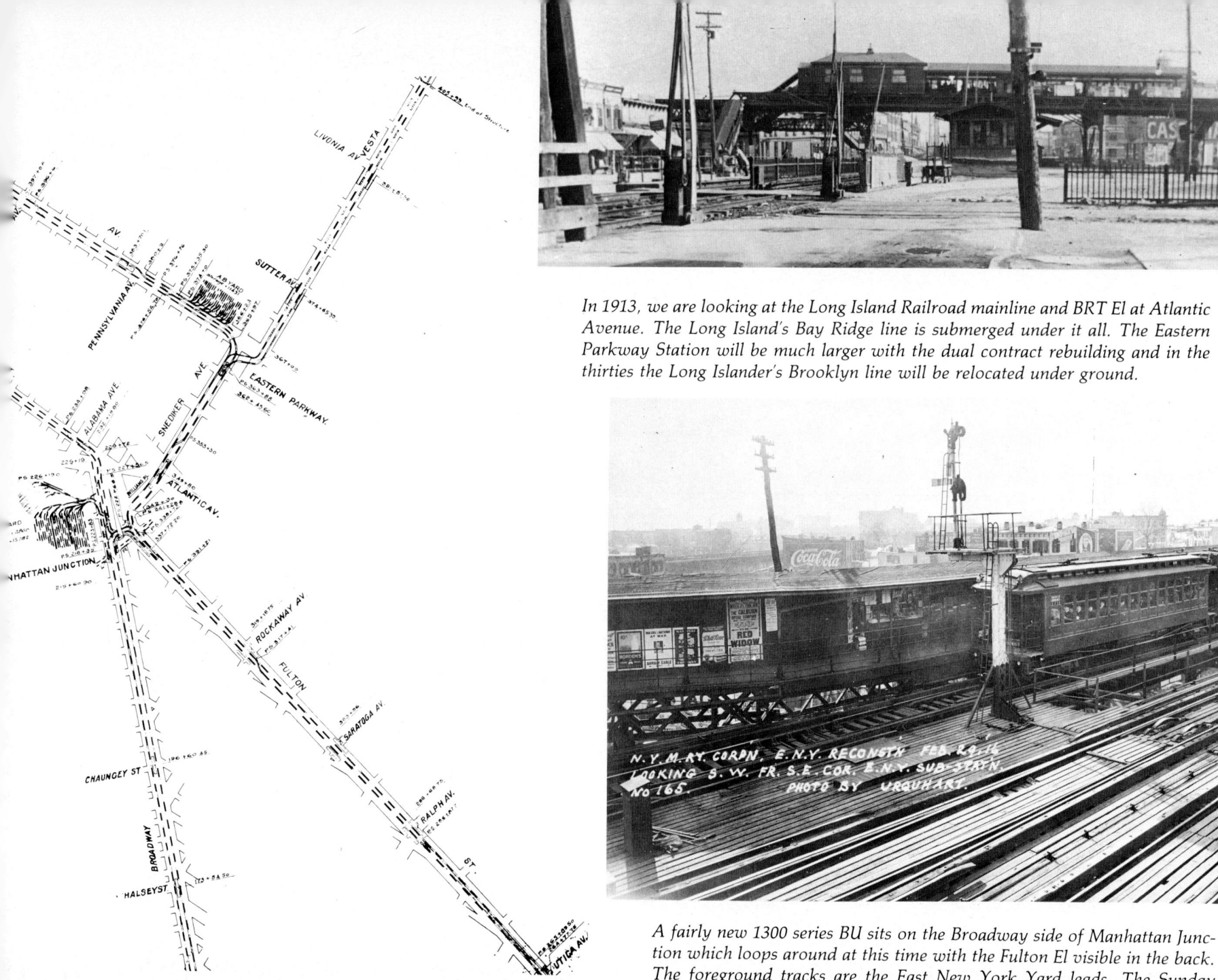

In 1913, we are looking at the Long Island Railroad mainline and BRT El at Atlantic Avenue. The Long Island's Bay Ridge line is submerged under it all. The Eastern Parkway Station will be much larger with the dual contract rebuilding and in the thirties the Long Islander's Brooklyn line will be relocated under ground.

A fairly new 1300 series BU sits on the Broadway side of Manhattan Junction which loops around at this time with the Fulton El visible in the back. The foreground tracks are the East New York Yard leads. The Sunday Eagle will have a lead story in this issue about The Rules of Nations at War. 1331 is a Lexington train headed for Cypress Hill in 1916 when America will head into a war.

88

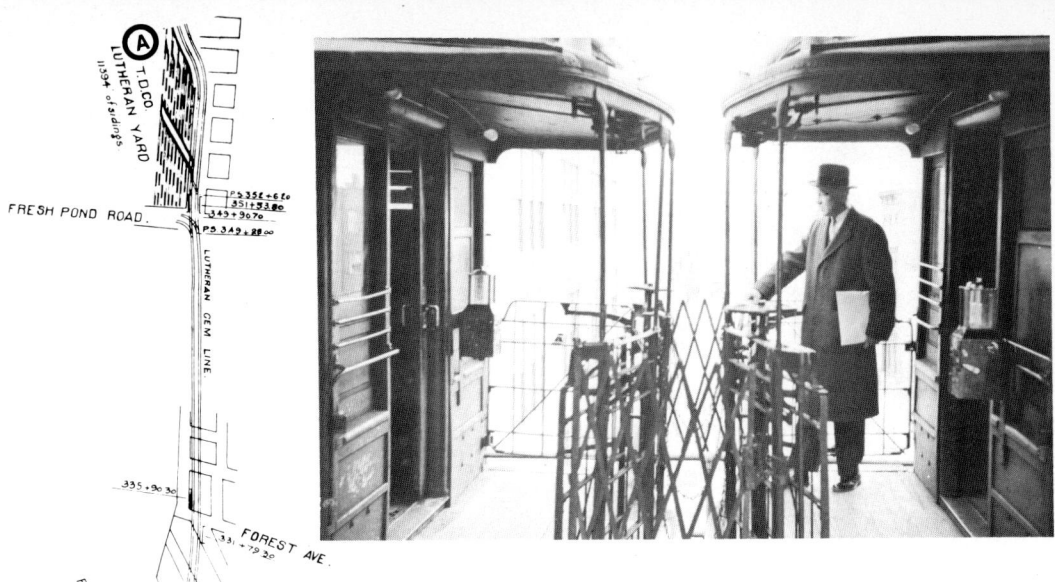

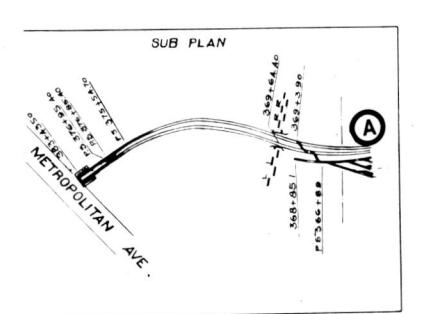

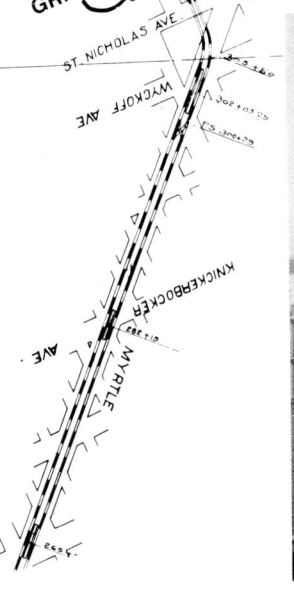

(Opposite Page Top Left) Fresh Pond Station at grade level in 1914. (Opposite Page Lower Left) The barn at Fresh Pond Road was used to service both elevated and surface cars. When the line is elevated to Fresh Pond Road and the trolley yard beyond the El yard is complete, only trolleys will use the barn. (Opposite Page Left) The Metropolitan Station and Tower in 1917. (Opposite Page Top) Fare boxes mounted on the platform were used on Sunday and at service night when El stations were closed and the conductor collected the fare. (Top Page) 1914 view of Fresh Pond with trolley yard in the background under construction. (Top Right) BU's on a fan trip show a yard full of Blue Bird's, Zephyr's, BU's and R16's. (Right) 1300's swing around the Wyckoff Avenue curve near the setting of their long career.

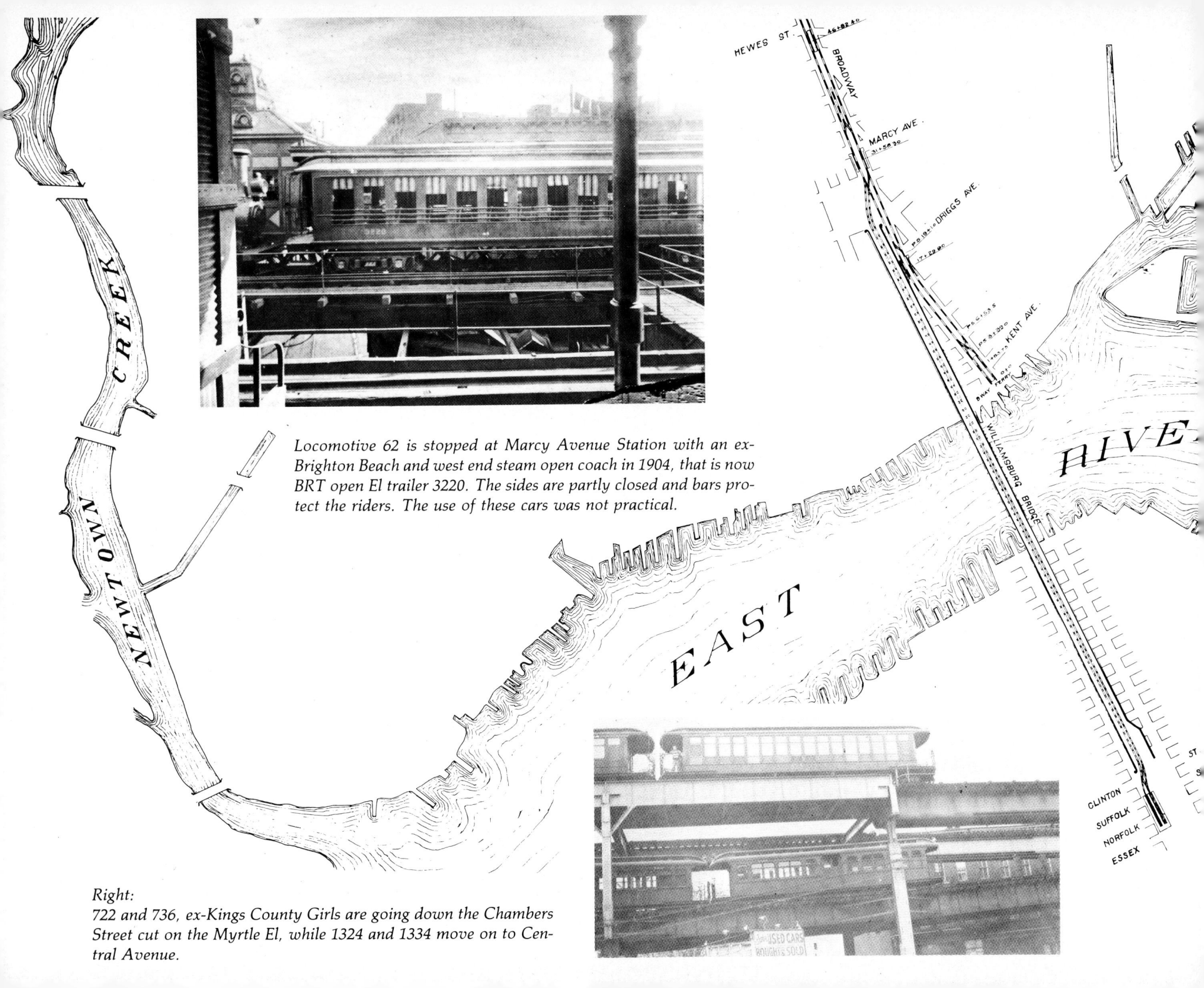

Locomotive 62 is stopped at Marcy Avenue Station with an ex-Brighton Beach and west end steam open coach in 1904, that is now BRT open El trailer 3220. The sides are partly closed and bars protect the riders. The use of these cars was not practical.

Right:
722 and 736, ex-Kings County Girls are going down the Chambers Street cut on the Myrtle El, while 1324 and 1334 move on to Central Avenue.

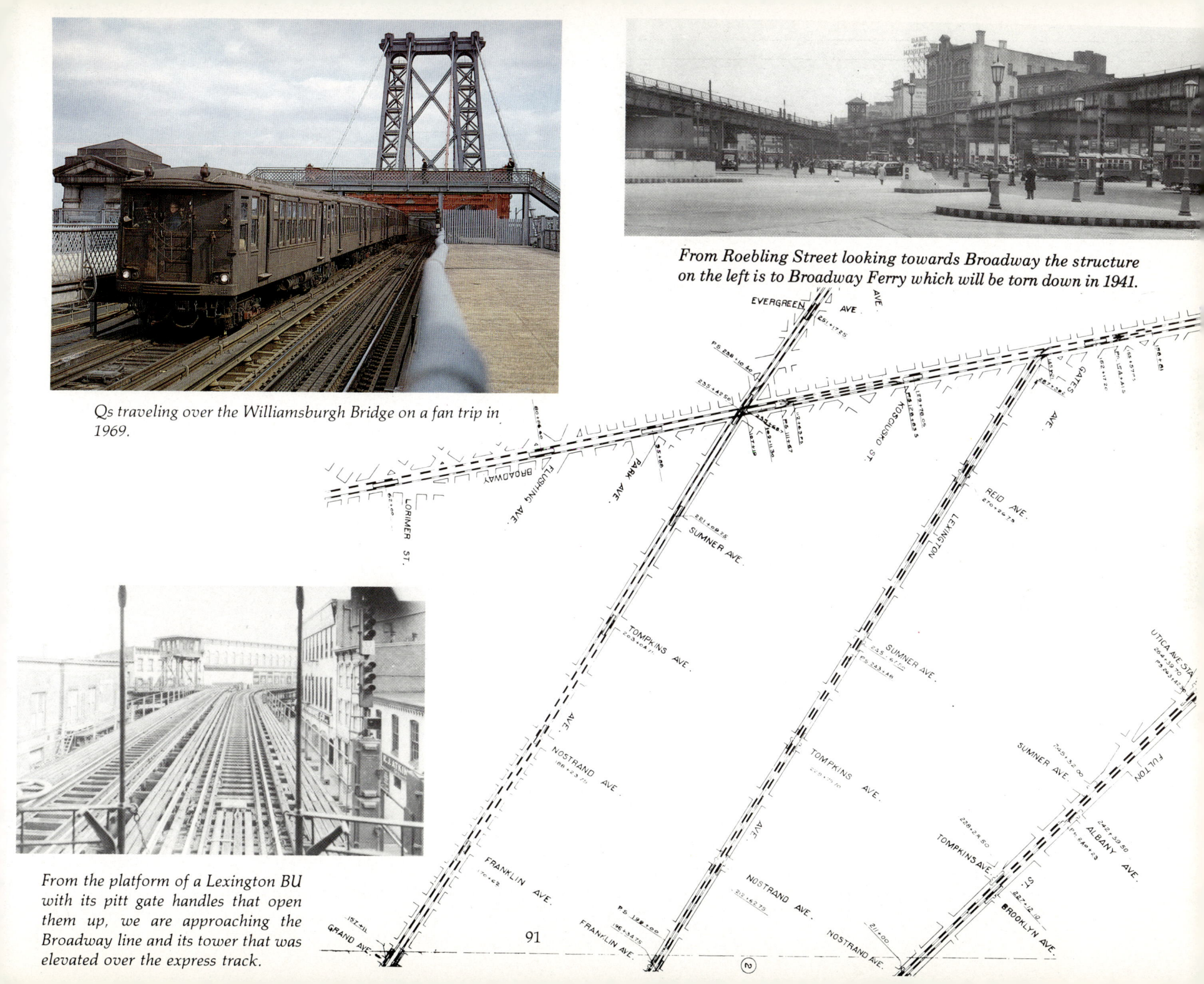

Qs traveling over the Williamsburgh Bridge on a fan trip in 1969.

From Roebling Street looking towards Broadway the structure on the left is to Broadway Ferry which will be torn down in 1941.

From the platform of a Lexington BU with its pitt gate handles that open them up, we are approaching the Broadway line and its tower that was elevated over the express track.

91

Broadway Elevated

(Top left) Broadway Elevated at Stone Avenue showing the columns of the old structure (in the street) and the newer wider structure moved curbside. *(Top right)* Cooper and Broadway. Note the Liebmann & Sons (Rheingold Beer) glass awnings. This was common-place then. Most of Broadway today is in ruins. The moving crane has reached the original Lexington connection to the Broadway line. H.C. Bohack Super Market sign is another lost piece of Brooklyn.

Myrtle Avenue Elevated

(Upper right) Broadway and Myrtle Avenues with wood temporary structure supporting the Myrtle line while a new local track structure is being put in. (Lower left) Moving crane used to hoist steel in place is at the end of the original island platform, which will soon become the Jamaica Express track. (Lower right) Standing on the old platform, the new local track structure is going up. Larger cranes behind tower will carry other pieces to their place. The tower above, still is use to this day, for Chamber Steet cut trains.

Fulton Street Elevated

(Top left) Fulton Street and Lewis Avenue, April 11, 1914. (Lower left) Brooklyn Avenue and the original simple wood stations of the Fulton El in the summertime. (Lower right) The Tomplains Avenue sub-station with a freight riding next to it, one cannot help but admire the clean and elaborate stores along the Avenue.

(Upper left) Utica Avenue station, looking East, as a small drew of workers are installing the new express tracks. The photographer, Urquhart, took many of the BRT photographs. This series shows the reconstruction of the elevated lines as part of the dual contract system. (Upper right) The large traveling crane was used to put new transverse girders to widen the line so it could have an express track installed. (Bottom) Out of the old structure, a new one emerges. (Summer Avenue Station) In the old days, they totally rebuilt the system, without interruption of service!

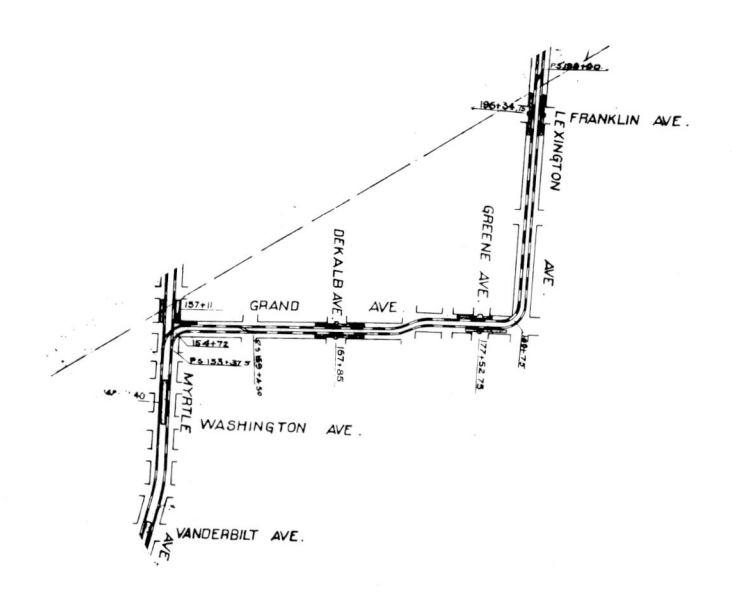

Looking down the Fifth Avenue line toward Fulton Street.

The wide Flatbush Avenue extension built for the new Manhattan Bridge which ends at the Fulton El in 1909.

A very meaningful area is Grand Street and Myrtle Avenue in the far right and between the foreground tracks we see the old connection to the Park Avenue El. The tracks to the left go off to Lexington Avenue line. The tower sits in the center of Grand and Myrtle.

Prospect Park Station of Brooklyn, Flatbush and Coney Island at Flatbush and Ocean Avenue in 1885.

The abandoned Union Street station of the 5th Avenue elevated with 2551 on the Union St. line.

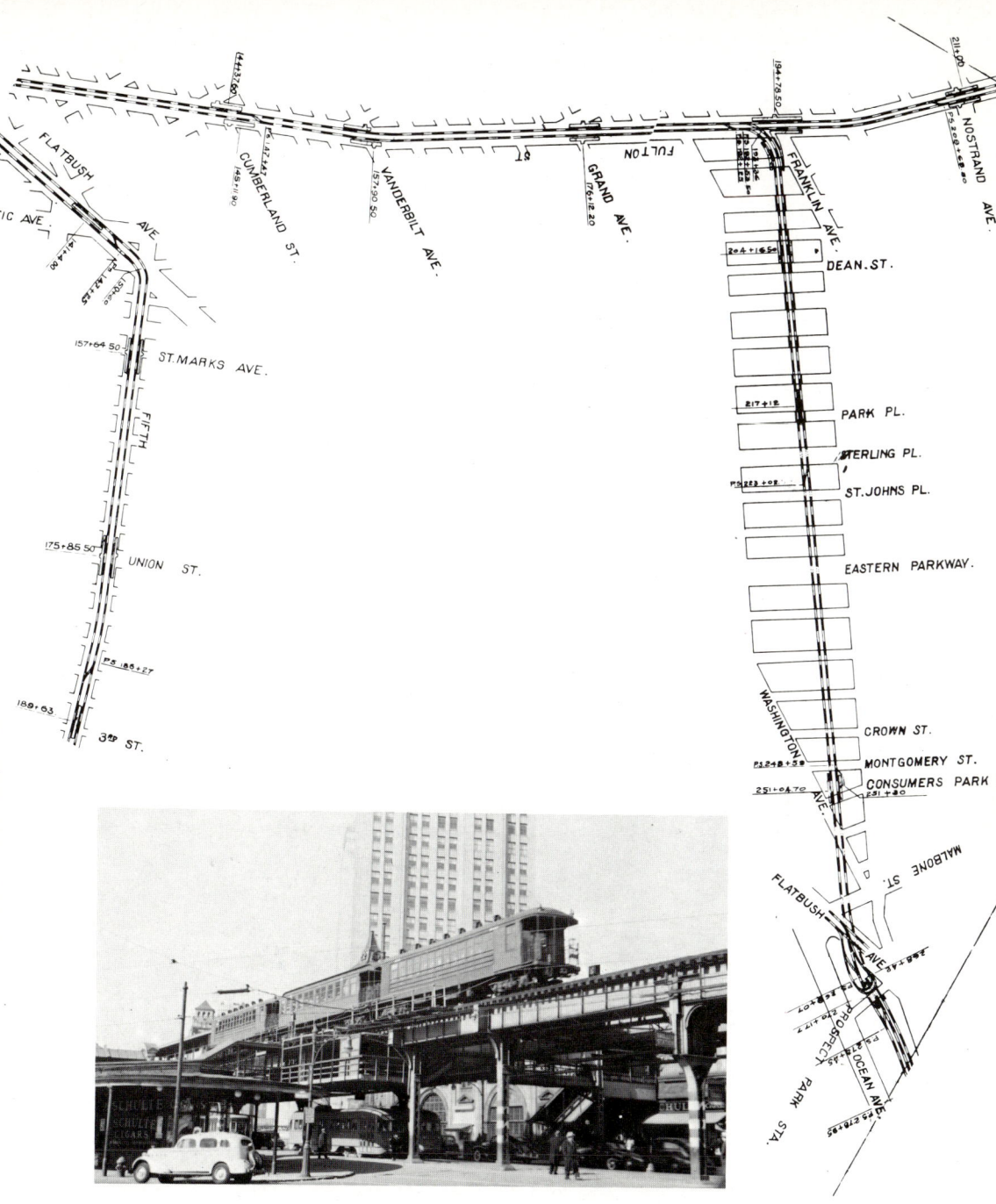

Culver line train of 1070; 97 and 1043 move up Flatbush Avenue near Long Island Station which once had a connection to the El at this point. Note PCC 1056 under El.

The rear of the Brighton Beach Hotel, a summer haven for many a summer season as seen from the Brighton Beach Station in 1916. The Brighton Beach Race Track is on the right.

It is the winter season and Dobbin has his coat on, otherwise the Phoenix Hotel at Sheepshead Bay would be a lot livelier than it is now. The slight wood platforms helped travelers get up those high El car steps. Piels, a Brooklyn beer, is served in the saloon across the street.

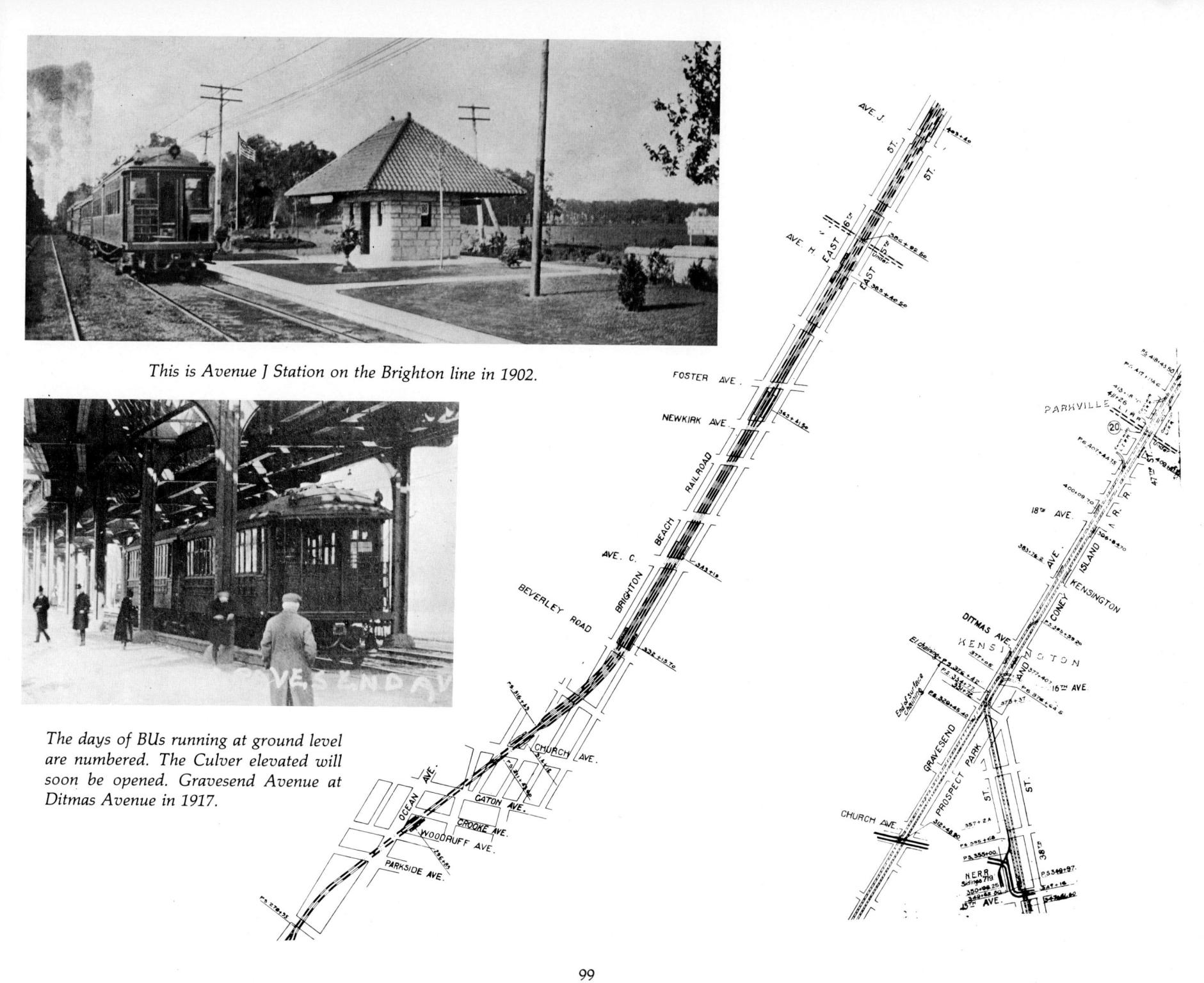

This is Avenue J Station on the Brighton line in 1902.

The days of BUs running at ground level are numbered. The Culver elevated will soon be opened. Gravesend Avenue at Ditmas Avenue in 1917.

99

859 and 821 have just brought in a load of fun seekers at Culver Terminal in 1913. Train after train all summer long carried the crowds from Bushwick, Williamsburg, Greenpoint, Ridgewood and perhaps Manhattan.

In the distance, a Brighton train is turning into the Culver Terminal using the old Sea View railroad's right of way. The far right shows the scenic railway car Number 9 and at least one guy holding onto his hat. These are our ancestors off to have a good time and memories that we may have heard about.

Stillwell Avenue Station is the heir of all the Coney Island terminals, pictured here in 1930. Coney Island looks more civilized but the fun and excitement of the earlier days is lost a little.

The West End terminal at Surf Avenue in 1912.

The reverse view of the Culver depot on the previous page.

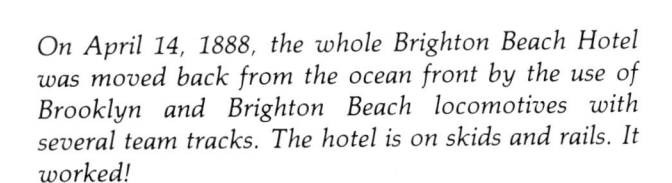

On April 14, 1888, the whole Brighton Beach Hotel was moved back from the ocean front by the use of Brooklyn and Brighton Beach locomotives with several team tracks. The hotel is on skids and rails. It worked!

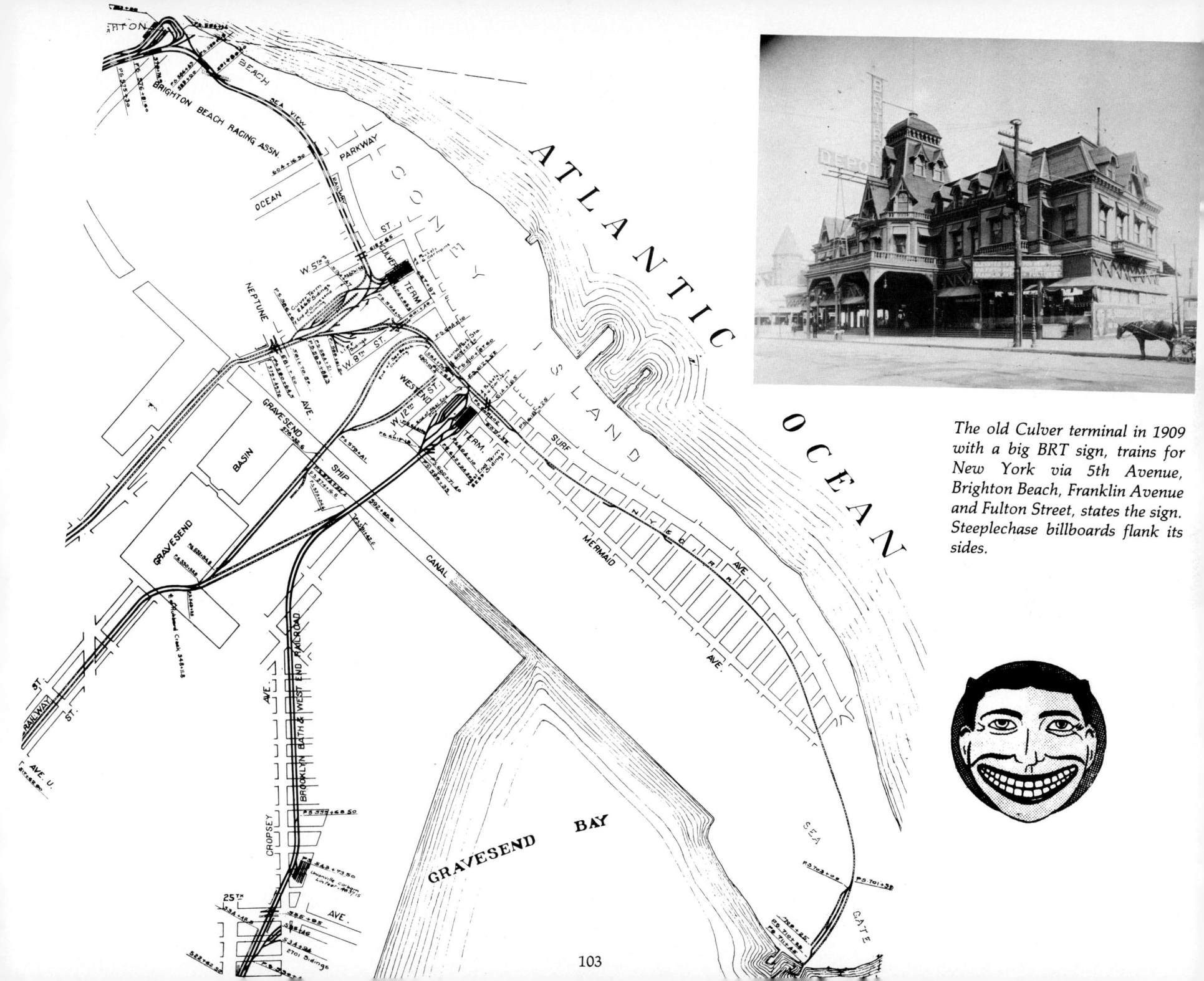

The old Culver terminal in 1909 with a big BRT sign, trains for New York via 5th Avenue, Brighton Beach, Franklin Avenue and Fulton Street, states the sign. Steeplechase billboards flank its sides.

This is 57th Street and New Utrech Avenue. You can see that the neighborhood could not take the heavy train traffic on the street much longer. The area between the ferry landing and Coney Island has grown up and fast.

A lone 1000 on the west end crossing the Sea Beach in 1914. The cut solved the crossing problem. The Sea Beach track on the left is part of the old grade crossing.

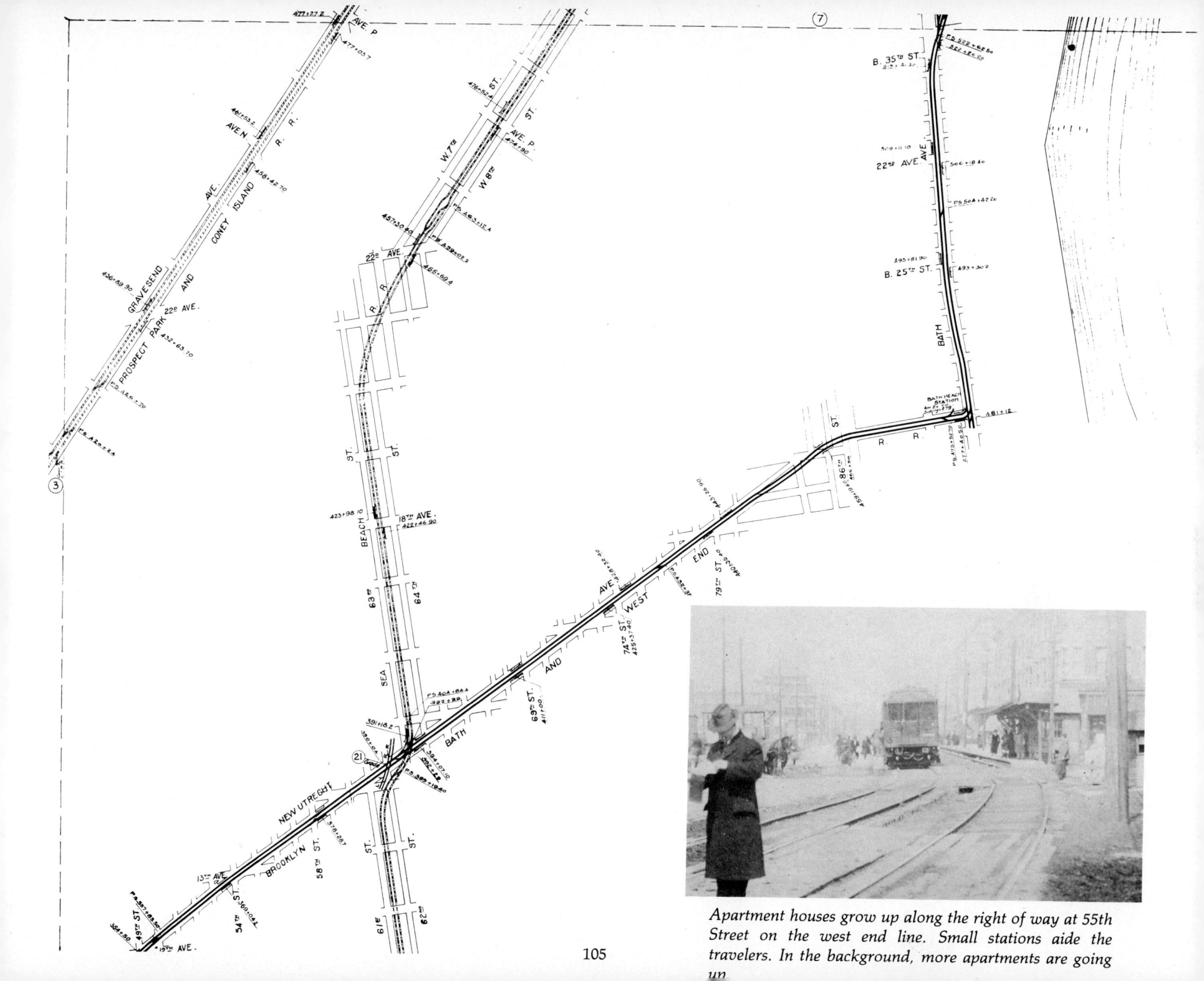

Apartment houses grow up along the right of way at 55th Street on the west end line. Small stations aide the travelers. In the background, more apartments are going up.

(Left) The celebration of the first electric train on the West End Line in 1900. (Bottom Left) Trailer 76 started life pulled by steam locomotives on this fan trip it is pulled up Second Avenue with electric locomotive No. 7. (Bottom) 65th Street Station with its lone 1000 series shuttle car.

106

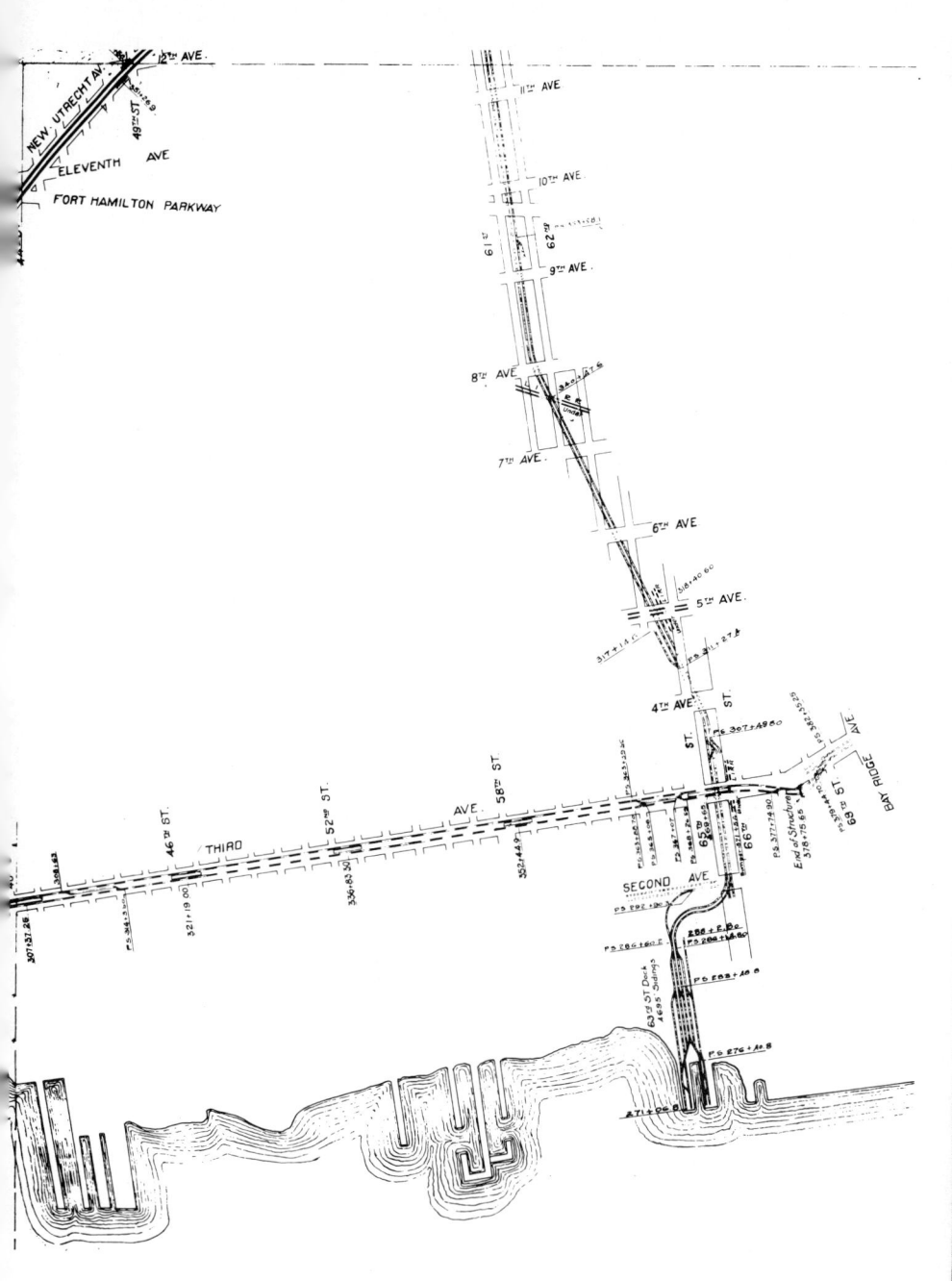

Looking north of 58th Street Station on Third Avenue.

Looking in the other direction of 65th Street Station, we can see the street car connection beyond the bumper. The trolley climbed the structure and passengers would walk forward to the El trains.

Perhaps the most important structure to the elevated story is the 39th Street shops. Before Coney Island shops, 39th Street was the heavy building and rebuilding shops of the BRT. Originally built as a large terminal shed for the South Brooklyn Railroad, it was never used for that purpose. In 1902, the BRT closed off the front with doors. The shop could hold 70 cars for shopping. Here the large fleet of aged steam coaches emerged as motor cars. In the photo above a shuttle car turns onto Third Avenue in 1940. (Top) The old 39th Street shops has become a bus garage. Today the exit ramp of the Brooklyn Queens Expressway occupies the space where so much rapid transit work took place.

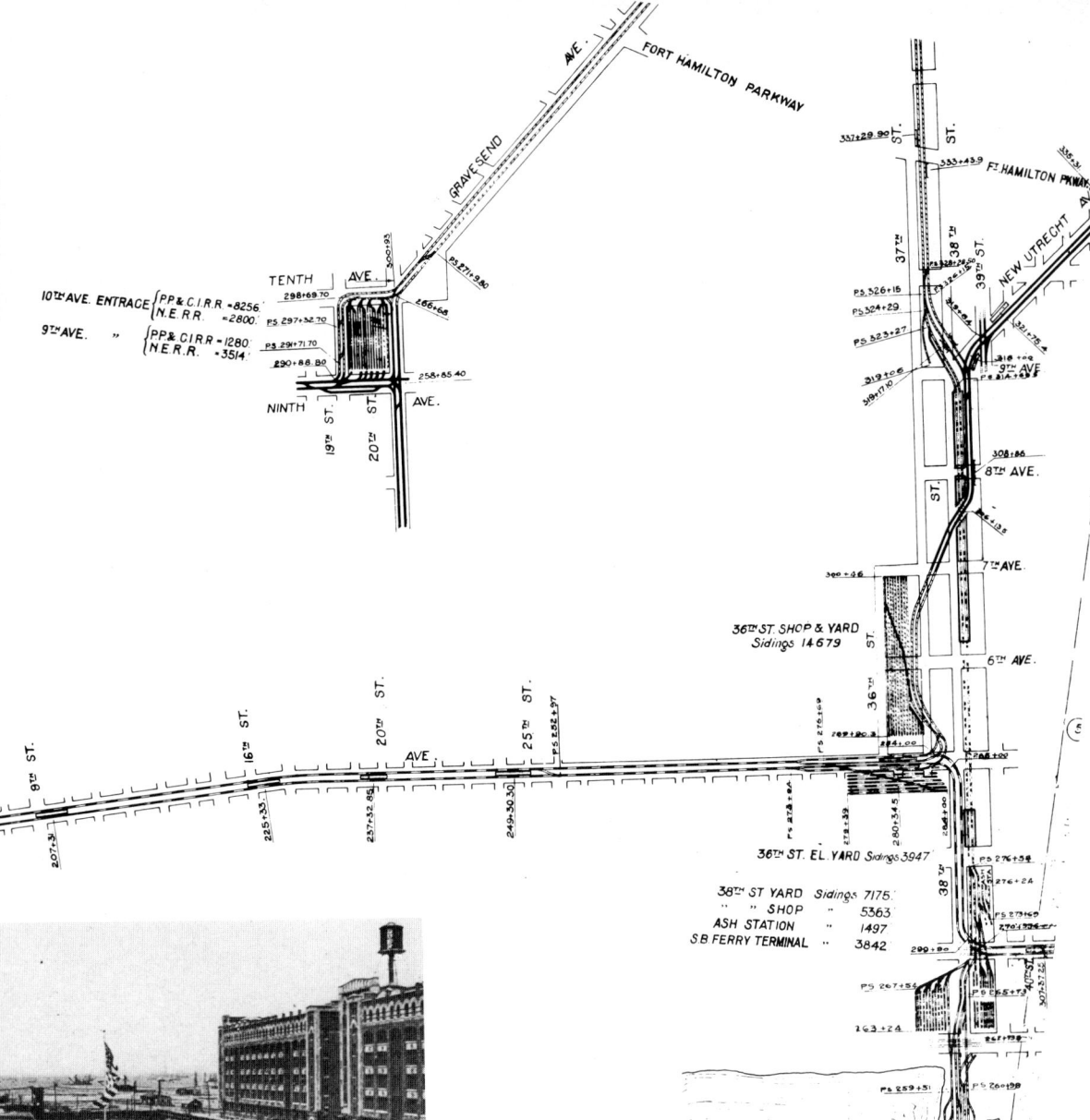

108

Top Right:
An aerial view of the same area. The steel structure to the left was once the steam engine yard, now just a skeleton. The Culver track turned to the right and the 36th Street shop building is behind it. It lasted until the 1980's as a bus garage when it was replaced.

Lower Left:
36th Street El shops in 1936; down the street is the Fifth Avenue El. In the shop one can see a new Multi and next to it, the Budd Zephyr Multi.

(Bottom)
A Third Avenue shuttle turns on to Fifth Avenue with the Culver tracks turning off to the left.

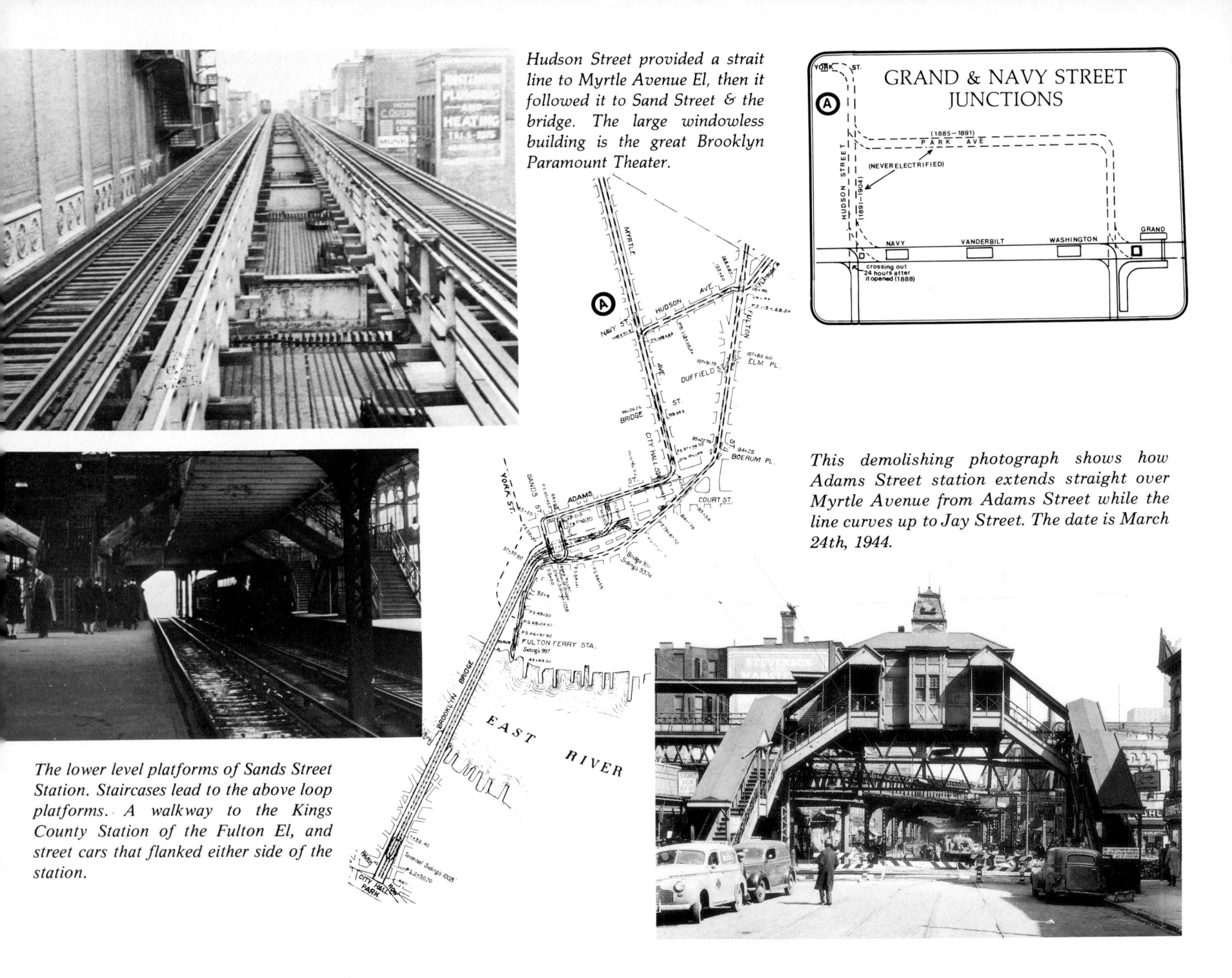

Hudson Street provided a strait line to Myrtle Avenue El, then it followed it to Sand Street & the bridge. The large windowless building is the great Brooklyn Paramount Theater.

GRAND & NAVY STREET JUNCTIONS

This demolishing photograph shows how Adams Street station extends straight over Myrtle Avenue from Adams Street while the line curves up to Jay Street. The date is March 24th, 1944.

The lower level platforms of Sands Street Station. Staircases lead to the above loop platforms. A walkway to the Kings County Station of the Fulton El, and street cars that flanked either side of the station.

Right:
8221 on Flatbush Avenue is stopped for a light. 930 at the end of a Culver train will stop at Fulton Street after crossing under the Fulton El. The steel structure of the 5th Avenue El contrasts with the thin cast iron and steel lattice work of the old Fulton Elevated.

Below:
A Culver train heads for Sands Street stop at Fulton Street Station, whose roof has small dormer windows crowned by a small chimney that must connect to a pot belly stove. The Brooklyn Paramont in the rear is now part of Long Island University.

Below Right:
Myrtle Avenue Stations are not directly in line with each other because Court Street crosses Fulton Street at an angle.

In this view, we see a train of C Type cars crossing onto the Fulton Street El from Sands Street. Note no Tillary Street Station. (See Photo Page 27) To the right is the Bridge Yard as it was called and the Tower for the Myrtle Avenue El connection and the yard itself.

We are standing on Washington Street looking northeast at the Sands Street structure. The trolley lines now share the station on their way to the bridge in 1911.

The Sands Street loop covers part of the Fulton El and the King County El spur. The long walkway connected to the bridge railway when they were separate but with the Fulton El trains running over the bridge, it was little used and like Fulton Ferry was abandoned.

From almost the bridge view of Sands Street before the trolley line also had a track built into Sands Street Station on our sections of the building. This eliminated a line up of cars along Washington Street, like you have in the photograph.

Above:
The loop tracks of Kings County terminal and Fulton Ferry are gone and a year from now so will the whole Sand Street structure.

Above Right:
So much transit history is here from cable car and steam to electric BU moving people. The Heights Theater on Washington Street is for sale or lease. Something on the great hustle and bussel of Brooklyn own downtown city is being distroyed here.

Below Right:
This dismantling of Park Row is the end of another fine way to travel around New York. Another two are also pictured on the left and will go.

113

998

In 1908 the Transit Development Corporation, a part of BRT, purchased one steel elevated car, No. 998. The car was built after a Boston elevated order of steel cars. 998 closely resembles the Boston car and like them was called "Easy Access Cars." The car had little success and was used as a shuttle car between Broadway Ferry to Marcy Avenue. It was stored and finally had a center door cut into its side for rubbish storage in Coney Island Yards. The car was scrapped in the early 60s.

Francis J. Goldsmith Jr. Collection

998 Brand New!

With center door as rubbish car at Coney Island

114

The 1930s were a time of depression but also a new age of designing. The BMT was a driving force in the field of transportation. The PCC was part of their trolley efforts and the first lightweight rapid transit car was another.

In 1934 with railroading parading Union Pacific's M-10000 and the Pioneer Zephyr, the BMT received from Pullman a five-car aluminum articulated train dubbed the Green Hornel and the Edward G. Budd Company built a five-car articulated stainless steel train dubbed the Zephyr. After testing in 1936 the management ordered 10 very different designs from St. Louis and 15 units from Pullman Standard. They were five-unit articulated sets dubbed Multi's by the crews. The depression effected design with indirect lighting giving way to bare bulbs. They also used automatic metal destination signs, with the city takeover nearing, the El lines like the trolley lines, were targeted for extinction. So the lightweight motors ran on the many curves of the 14th Street Canarsie line. The Multi's were so lightweight they could run over the Fulton El from Eastern Parkway to Lefferts Ave. Thus the 14th Street-Fulton line. In 1939, the last and most spectacular of these articulateds were five sets (3 cars in each set) built by the Clark Equipment Company. The car sets were painted 2 tone blue and white. They were dubbed "The Blue Bird." They were small but had bulls eye lighting, mohair seats, tile on the floors and the use of mirrors in the interior design. They ran on PCC trucks. These little orphans were left to run on the Eastern Division until the late 50s. The Green Hornet was scrapped during the war for its aluminum. The Hornet was not equipped with couplers. These cars were exciting to ride. The Multi's were the only cars where the passenger load out weighed the train, and so they could move and stop on a dime, something the passengers did not enjoy. The management had big signs stating "Hold On." You could sit in the end car and watch the train snake around curves at a good clip. None of these important and wonderful trains were saved.

The aluminum Green Hornet at Coney Island. Green Hornet interior was a decor dream.

115

Called the Little Zephyr, the Little Zephyr could not MU with any other Multi-Units. The pleasant interior used indirect lighting, similar to the Green Hornet. The Zephyr was Budd's first step into the field of rapid transit. The Zephyr worked on the Franklin Shuttle and the rest of her years on the Eastern Division.

Clarks Manufacturing, builder of thousands of P.C.C. trucks, only made one bid in manufacture equipment and the Blue Bird was it. The interior of the Blue Birds made them one of the most advanced cars of their time. Mirrors, boarding the car's passage ways, gave a more open look to the cars. Mohair cushioning and P.C.C. bulls-eye lighting sets a very comfortable tone to the interiors.

Fresh Pond Yard in 1956.

116

Multi at Lefferts Avenue station on the Fulton El.

Brand new at Canarsie depot.

THE MULT'S

Van Siclan station of Fulton El.

Multi, crossing Rockaway Beach line of the Long Island R.R.

ROSTER OF BRT ELEVATED EQUIPMENT

CAR #	BUILDER	DATE	OWNER	SEAT TYPE	NOTES
1-51	PULLMAN	1884	B.E.R.R.	Man. TR	Cars 30,35-44 Cross seating
52-132	GILBERT & BUSH	1887	U.E.R.R.	Cr. TR	Cars 57,62,70-132 Long. seating
133-137	PULLMAN	1891	B.E.R.R.	Man. TR	Note#3
138-190	OSGOOD BRADLEY	1893	SS & B.B.	Man. TR	Note#3
191-256	PULLMAN	1888-9	K.C.E.R.R.	Man. TR	197 at Branford Museum
257-271	HARLAN & HARLINGSWORTH	1893	K.C.E.R.R.	Cr. TR	
600-601	GILBERT & BUSH	1887	U.E.R.R.	Long. MTR	Note#A Note#2 Note#3
602-614	PULLMAN	1891	B.E.R.R.	Man. MTR	Note#4
615-619	OSGOOD BRADLEY	1893	SS & B.B.	Man. MTR	Note#5
620-627	PULLMAN	1898	B.E.R.R.	Long. MTR	Note#A Note#6
628-632	BRILL	1900	B.U.	Cr. MTR	Note#7
633-682	JEWETT	1901	B.U.	Man-semi MTR	Note#8 659 at Branford Museum
683	GILBERT & BUSH	1887	U.E.R.R.	Long. MTR	Note#3
684	GILBERT & BUSH	1887	U.E.R.R.	Long. MTR	Note#3 Note#9
695	PULLMAN	1884	B.E.R.R.	MTR	Work car with large center door added. Note#1
696-699	PULLMAN	1898	SV.R.R.	MTR	Work cars Note#10
700-758	PULLMAN	1888	K.C.E.R.R.	Long. MTR	Note#A
759-760	GILBERT & BUSH	1887	U.E.R.R.	Long. MTR	Note#A Note#11
800-832	PULLMAN	1884	B.E.R.R.	Long. MTR	Note#A Note#1 Note#12
833-858	GILBERT & BUSH	1887	U.E.R.R.	Long. MTR	Note#A Note#3
859	OSGOOD BRADLEY	1893	SS & B.B.	Long. MTR	Note#A Note#13
900-935	WASON	1898	K.C.E.R.R.	Long. MTR	Note#14 Built with center door
936	PULLMAN	1888	K.C.E.R.R.	Long. MTR	Note#15
937-940	BRILL	1900	B.U.	Cr. MTR	Note#16
988-997	WORK CARS REBUILT FROM VARIOUS PASSENGER CARS				
998	PRESSED STEEL	1908	T.D.C.	Man. MTR	Steel car. Center door added in 1946 for rubbish storage
999	BKLYN. HEIGHTS R.R.	1905	T.D.C.		MTR. Instruction car Branford
1000-1119	STEPHENSON	1902	T.D.C.	Cr.	MTR. Convertible
1200-1234	OSGOOD BRADLEY	1903	T.D.C.	Man.	MTR. 1227 at Branford
1235-1259	BRILL	1903	T.D.C.	Man.	MTR.
1260-1299	LACONIA	1903	T.D.C.	Man.	MTR.
1300-1349	CINCINNATI	1905	T.D.C.	Cr.	MTR. Convertible
1350-1374	JEWETT	1905	T.D.C.	Cr.	MTR. Convertible
1375-1399	LACONIA	1905	T.D.C.	Cr.	MTR. Convertible Note#17
1400-1449	JEWETT	1907	T.D.C.	Man.	MTR.
1450-1499	LACONIA	1907	T.D.C.	Man.	MTR.
1500-1501	BMT	1923	NYRT	Long.	"C" Note#19
1502-1526	BMT	1925	NYRT	Man.	"C" Note#19
1600-1629	BMT	1838-39	NYRT	Man.	"Q" Note#20
1630-1642	BMT	1939	NYRT	Man.	"QX" Note#21
3200-3225	VARIOUS	1879-1881	NY&SB	Bench	TR Note#18
3226-3233	WASON	1892	BB&WE	Bench	TR Note#18
3235	WASON	1895	BB&WE	Bench	MTR Large open Bench open

3200 series were originally BRT surface numbers, transferred to elevated lines in 1900. All scrapped in 1905.

Note#A, Center door added
Note#1, Same as trailer type 1-51
Note#2, Ex 448-449
Note#3, Same as trailer type 52-132
Note#4, Same as trailer type 133-137
Note#5, Same as trailer type 138-190
Note#6, Ex400-411 Built as Motor cars
Note#7, Ex436-440 renumbered in 1930 as 937-940
Note#8, Ex450-499
Note#9, Became 1261 in 1930
Note#10, Ex432-435 699 ex 432 rebuilt to open in 1901 in 1906 rebuilt to rubbish car 994
Note#11, 759ex850 760ex852
Note#12, 817 rebuilt by T.D.C. in 1909 became 1282 in 1930
Note#13, Same type car as 615-615
Note#14, Ex500-540
Note#15, Ex541
Note#16, Ex628-632
Note#17, 1362 & 1349 at Branford 1365 at St. Louis Museum of Transportation
Note#18, Open bench steam trailers rebuilt to run as open elevated trailer
Note#19, 3-unit A-B-C units, A&C cars made from 12 & 1400s series BUs and Bunits made from 138-190 series trailers. Only units with door in center are 1500 & 1501 (List A)
Note# 20, 3-unit A-B-C units all made from 12 & 1400s series BUs. (List B)
Note# 21, 2-unit A-B cars all made from 12-1400 series BUs. (List C)

KEY TO ABBREVIATIONS

B.E.R.R. .... BROOKLYN ELEVATED RAILROAD
B.U.R.R. .... BROOKLYN UNION ELEVATED RAILROAD
B.B.&W.E. .... BRIGHTON BEACH & WEST END RAILROAD
K.C.R.R. .... KINGS COUNTY RAILROAD
N.Y.R.T. .... NEW YORK RAPID TRANSIT
N.Y.&S.B. .... NEW YORK & SEA BEACH
S.S.&B.B. .... SEASIDE & BROOKLYN BRIDGE
S.V.R.R. .... SEAVIEW RAILROAD
T.D. .... TRANSIT DEVELOPMENT CORPORATION
U.E.R.R. .... UNION ELEVATOR RAILROAD

BRT ELECTRIC LOCOMOTIVES

LOCOMOTIVES	BUILDER	DATE	TYPE	NOTES
No. 1	BKLYN.HEIGHTS R.R.	1904	STEEPLE CAB	Scrapped 1955 VD type Couplers
No. 2	BKLYN.HEIGHTS R.R.	1904	STEEPLE CAB	Scrapped 1944 VD type Couplers
No. 3	BKLYN.HEIGHTS R.R.	1904	STEEPLE CAB	Scrapped 1954 VD type Couplers
No. 4	BKLYN.HEIGHTS R.R.	1907	BOX TYPE	Branford Museum MCB Couplers
No. 5	GE/AMERICAN LOCOMOTIVE	1910	STEEPLE CAB	Transit Museum MCB Couplers
No. 6	GENERAL ELECTRIC	1921	STEEPLE CAB	Transit Museum MCB&WH Couplers
No. 7	GENERAL ELECTRIC	1925-26	STEEPLE CAB	Transit Museum MCB&WH Couplers

LIST A
C TYPE CARS

A UNIT	B UNIT	C UNIT	A UNIT	B UNIT	C UNIT
1500	1496	188	1497	1500	1514	1460	172	1461	1514
1501	1498	189	1499	1501	1515	1458	170	1459	1515
1502	1468	176	1469	1502	1516	1472	178	1473	1516
1503	1478	181	1479	1503	1517	1454	168	1455	1517
1504	1470	177	1471	1504	1518	1466	175	1467	1518
1505	1450	166	1451	1505	1519	1480	182	1481	1519
1506	1485	184	1486	1506	1520	1488	185	1489	1520
1507	1492	187	1493	1507	1521(1)	1490	186	1491	1521(1)
1508	1494	190	1495	1508	1521(2)	1490	164	1491	1521(2)
1509(1)	1483	183	1484	1509(1)	1522	1476	180	1477	1522
1509(2)	1483	146	1484	1509(2)	1523	1422	167	1423	1523
1510	1462	173	1463	1510	1524	1286	159	1287	1524
1511	1464	174	1465	1511	1525	1282	157	1283	1525
1512	1474	179	1475	1512	1526(1)	1260	146	1261	1526(1)
1513	1456	169	1457	1513	1526(2)	1260	183	1261	1526(2)

LIST B
Q TYPE CARS

A UNIT	B UNIT	C UNIT
1600A(1) ex-1267,	1600B ex-1211,	1600C ex-1409

In July 1950, 1600A(I) was renumbered 1641 (II) & the original 1641A ex-1264 became 1600A (II). It was felt that 1641A was the better car to be sent as 1600A for use on the 3rd. Avenue El.

1601A ex-1433,	1601B ex-1243,	1601C ex-1427
1602A ex-1410,	1602B ex-1272,	1602C ex-1405
1603A ex-1419,	1603B ex-1252,	1603C ex-1404 ●
1604A ex-1232,	1604B ex-1207,	1604C ex-1247

Q TYPE CARS

A UNIT		B UNIT		C UNIT	
1605A	ex-1447,	1605B	ex-1239,	1605C	ex-1418
1606A	ex-1426,	1606B	ex-1202,	1606C	ex-1435
1607A	ex-1453,	1607B	ex-1223,	1607C	ex-1429
1608A	ex-1428,	1608B	ex-1241,	1608C	ex-1403
1609A	ex-1406,	1609B	ex-1225,	1609C	ex-1408
1610A	ex-1412,	1610B	ex-1218,	1610C	ex-1449
1611A	ex-1416,	1611B	ex-1275,	1611C	ex-1434
1612A	ex-1432,	1612B	ex-1292,	1612C	ex-1417
1613A	ex-1424,	1613B	ex-1263,	1613C	ex-1401
1614A	ex-1425,	1614A	ex-1216,	1614C	ex-1442
1615A	ex-1278,	1615B	ex-1269,	1615C	ex-1436
1616A	ex-1290,	1616B	ex-1244,	1616C	ex-1441
1617A	ex-1421,	1617C	ex-1242,	1617C	ex-1277
1618A	ex-1248,	1618B	ex-1266,	1618C	ex-1452
1619A	ex-1413,	1619B	ex-1251,	1619C	ex-1437
1620A	ex-1438,	1620B	ex-1224,	1620C	ex-1439
1621A(I)	ex-1411,	burned	Feb. 1943		replaced
1621A(II)	ex-1213,	1621B	ex-1268,	1621C	ex-1446
1622A	ex-1407, ●	1622B	ex-1273, ●	1622C	ex-1265
1623A	ex-1255,	1623B	ex-1250,	1623C	ex-1259
1624A	ex-1295,	1624B	ex-1274,	1624C	ex-1258
1625A	ex-1297,	1625B	ex-1230,	1625C	ex-1234
1626A	ex-1262,	1626B	ex-1280,	1626C	ex-1296
1627A	ex-1293,	1627B	ex-1257,	1627C	ex-1294
1628A	ex-1289,	1628B	ex-1284,	1628C	ex-1291
1629A	ex-1298,	1629B	ex-1236,	1629C	ex-1299

LIST C
QX TYPE CAR

A UNIT		B UNIT	
1630A	ex-1400,	1630B	ex-1231
1631A	ex-1402,	1631B	ex-1221
1632A	ex-1414,	1632B	ex-1233
1633A	ex-1444,	1633B	ex-1226
1634A	ex-1445,	1634B	ex-1270
1635A	ex-1430,	1635B	ex-1245
1636A	ex-1415,	1636B	ex-1209
1637A	ex-1420,	1637B	ex-1238
1638A	ex-1431,	1638B	ex-1222
1639A	ex-1443,	1639B	ex-1200
1640A	ex-1440,	1640B	ex-1204
1641A	ex-1264,	1641B	ex-1203
1642A	ex-1288,	1642B	ex-1256 renumbered 1643

● *Re-rebuilt back to open platform cars.*